JAVA ESSEN
FOR CLASS X ICSE

JAVA HANDBOOK

RANJIT SINGH

INDIA · SINGAPORE · MALAYSIA

Notion Press

Old No. 38, New No. 6
McNichols Road, Chetpet
Chennai - 600 031

First Published by Notion Press 2019
Copyright © Ranjit Singh 2019
All Rights Reserved.

ISBN 978-1-64733-648-6

CONTENTS

Abstract　　　　　　　　　　　　　　　　5

Acknowledgments　　　　　　　　　　　7

Sample Paper 1　　　　　　　　　　　　11

Solution Sample Paper 1　　　　　　　15

Sample Paper 2　　　　　　　　　　　　25

Solution Sample Paper 2　　　　　　　29

Sample Paper 3　　　　　　　　　　　　39

Solution Sample Paper 3　　　　　　　43

Sample Paper 4　　　　　　　　　　　　53

Solution Sample Paper 4　　　　　　　59

Sample Paper 5　　　　　　　　　　　　70

Solution Sample Paper 5　　　　　　　74

Sample Paper 6　　　　　　　　　　　　83

Solution Sample Paper 6　　　　　　　89

Sample Paper 7　　　　　　　　　　　　99

Solution Sample Paper 7　　　　　　　103

Sample Paper 8　　　　　　　　　　　　112

Solution Sample Paper 8　　　　　　　116

Sample Paper 9	126
Solution Sample Paper 9	129
Sample Paper 10	139
Solution Sample Paper 10	143
Sample Paper 11	152
Solution Sample Paper 11	157
Sample Paper 12	168
Solution Sample Paper 12	173

ABSTRACT

This book is designed for class X students ICSE stream. They can go through this book for challenging themselves with the questions which can be asked in the ICSE board examination. Students who are in the X standard or students who are going to enter in X standard, they will be highly benefited from this book. This book is designed based on the idea of all the questions compiled from the different Schools across India.

The idea of solving the questions which are asked in the multiple schools and challenging your concepts based on that what you have learnt it will be a good exercise. All the programs written in this book are compiled in BlueJ environment. Students are requested to copy the program in the BlueJ editor and run. You can change the input values to know how output is varying. It will help in understanding the logic behind it.

By the time you finish this book you will be an expert in solving any type of questions related to JAVA based on ICSE board pattern.

ACKNOWLEDGMENTS

I would like to thank my wife Vibha and two daughters Ritika and Risha for their patience, hard work and perseverance. Siddarth Kashyap Rudrabhatla, one of my students who helped me in collating all the answers. Without their support it would not have been possible. Further I would like to thank all my students whom I could help in writing their board exams for ICSE, their answers and hard work helped me in writing this book. Whole idea of presenting this book to bigger set of crowd is to let everyone succeed in making their understanding clear and work towards achieving their goals. If they can secure centum in board exam 2019 by following this pattern and clearing all the doubts anyone who wants to clarify their doubts and wants to secure their targets can read and get going. I promise this work which I have put together will reach to all the students who not only wants to secure good marks but want to do in understandable way. We believe you in your caliber and we want you to succeed. We put the path designed for you to follow and we wish you all the best.

ICSE
SAMPLE PAPER
FOR
CLASS X

Computer Application

SAMPLE PAPER 1

SECTION A   **(40 Marks)**

Attempt all questions

Question 1

(a) Name any four tokens of Java. [2]

(b) Give the difference between actual parameter and formal parameter. [2]

(c) What is an identifier? [2]

(d) Write an expression in Java for $\sin x + \sqrt{a^2 + b^3}$. [2]

(e) What is the result produced by 2 – 10*3 + 100/11? Show the steps. [2]

Question 2

(a) What is the difference between local variable and instance variable? [2]

(b) int x = 20, y = 10, z;

What is the value of z in

z = ++x * (y – –) – y ?

Show the steps. [2]

(c) What is the purpose of default in a switch? [2]

(d) Give the difference between linear search and binary search. [2]

(e) What will be the output of the following code?

```
float x = 7.87;
System.out.println(Math.ceil(x));
System.out.println(Math.floor(x)); [2]
```

Question 3

(a) State the difference between if-else if ladder and switch…case. [2]

(b) Explain the concept of constructor overloading with an example. [2]

(c) What will be the output of the following program segments?

(i) String s = "application";
int p = s.indexOf('a');
System.out.println(p);
System.out.println(p+s); [2]

(ii) String st = "PROGRAM";
System.out.println(st.indexOf(st.charAt(4))); [2]

(iii) int a = 0;
if(a>0 && a<20)
a++;
else a-- ;
System.out.println(a); [2]

(iv) int a= 5, b = 2,c;
if (a>b || a! = b)
c = ++a+--b;
System.out.print(c+ " "+a+ " "+b); [2]

(v) int i = 1;
while(i++<=1)
{
i++;
System.out.print(i + " ");
}
System.out.print(i); [2]

(d) Differentiate between isUpperCase(char) and toUpperCase(char). [2]

(e) What is the difference between a constructor function and a member function of a class? [2]

(f) What is the difference between a static member function and a member function which is not static? [2]

SECTION B   (60 Marks)

Attempt any four questions from this Section

The answers in this Section should consist of the Programs in either Blue J environment or any program environment with Java as the base. Each program should be written using Variable descriptions/Mnemonic Codes such that the logic of the program is clearly depicted.

Flow-Charts and Algorithms are not required.

Question 4

Define a class taximeter having the following description:

Data members/instance variables

int taxino – to store taxi number

String name – to store passenger's name

int km – to store number of kilometres travelled

Member functions:

taximeter() – constructor to initialize taxino to 0, name to " "and b to 0.

input() – to store taxino,name,km

calculate() – to calculate bill for a customer according to given conditions

kilometers travelled(km) Rate/km

kilometers travelled(km)	Rate/km
<1 km	Rs. 25
1 < km < 6	Rs. 10
6 < km < 12	Rs. 15
12 < km < 18	Rs. 20
>18 km	Rs. 25

display() – To display the details in the following format

Taxino Name Kilometres travelled Bill amount

- - - -

Create an object in the main method and call all the above methods in it. [15]

Question 5

Write a menu driven program to find the sum of the following series depending on the user choosing 1 or 2

1. S=1/4+1/8+1/12.........upto n terms

2. S=1/1!–2/2!+3/3!......upto n terms

where ! stands for factorial of the number and the factorial value of a number is the product of all integers from 1 to that number, e.g. 5! = 1* 2* 3* 4* 5.

(use switch-case). [15]

Question 6

Write a program to accept a sentence and print only the first letter of each word of the sentence in capital letters separated by a full stop.

Example:

INPUT SENTENCE : "This is a cat"

OUTPUT : T.I.A.C. [15]

Question 7

Write a program to create an array to store 10 integers and print the largest integer and the smallest integer in that array. [15]

Question 8

Write a program to calculate the sum of all the prime numbers between the range of 1 and 100. [15]

Question 9

Write a program to store 10 names in an array. Arrange these in alphabetical order by sorting. Print the sorted list. Take single word names, all in capital letters,

E.g. SAMSON, AJAY, LUCY, etc. [15]

SOLUTION SAMPLE PAPER 1

SECTION A   (40 Marks)

Answer 1

(a) Integer, boolean, double and character.

(b) Formal parameters are used in the function definition and Actual parameters are used when function is being called. E.g.

```
void sum(int a, int b) // a and b are formal parameters
  {
  System.out.println(a+b);
  }
Public static void main()
  {
  Sum(2,4) ; // 2, 4 are actual parameters.
  }
```

(c) Identifiers are names of the variables, strings, classes and packages. Its values can change throughout the program.

(d) Math.sin(x) + Math.sqrt(a*a + b*b*b);

(e) Step 1: $2 - 10*3 + 9$

Step 2: $3 - 30+9$

Step 3: $3 - 21$

Step 4: -19

Answer 2

(a)

Local Variable	Instance Variable
Its scope remains inside a function or the block.	Its scope remains throughout the methods of the class.
Multiple copies of this variable are used throughout the program.	Every object has separate copies of this variable.

(b) int x =20, y = 10, z;

z = ++x * (y – –) – y ?

Step 1: 21 * 10 – 9

Step 2: 210 – 9

Step 3: 201

(c) Default in the switch statement means when no matching case is encountered by the controller it executes the default case.

(d)

Linear Search	Binary Search
It compares each element of the array with rest of the elements in the array.	It's based on divide and conquer rule. Array is sorted in this search. Element is searched only in the selected halves.

e. 8.0
  7.0

Answer 3

(a)

If-else Ladder	Switch Case
Works on more than one variable	It works on only one variable or constant
It can hold many conditions	It can hold only one condition.

(b) Function name same as that of class name without return type is called Constructor. Constructor overloading is when same name constructor is used with different arguments list is called constructor overloading.

Example:

Class lol

{

lol ()

{

//write something …

}

lol(int a)

{

//write something

}

lol(int a, int b)

{

//write something

}

(c) (i) 0application

   (ii) 1

   (iii) −1

   (iv) 7 6 1

   (v) 34

(d)

isUpperCase()	toUpperCase()
It checks whether the character is uppercase or not.	It changes the character into uppercase
Return value is boolean.	Return value is String

(e)

Constructor Function	Member Function
Automatically called during the creation of the object.	Class object needs to explicitly call the member functions.
It bears the same name as that of class.	It doesn't have same name.

(f)

Static Member Function	Non Static Member Function
It has the keyword static before the function name.	It doesn't have static keyword before the function name.
It can be called by static member functions only.	It can be called by any function.

SECTION B   (60 Marks)

Answer 4

```java
import java.util.*;
class taximeter
   {
   int taxino;
   String name;
   int km;
   double fare;
   public taximeter()
      {
      taxino = 0;
      name =" ";
      km = 0;
      fare = 0.0;
      }
   public void input()
      {
      Scanner sc = new Scanner(System.in);
```

```
System.out.println("Enter taxi number");
taxino = sc.nextInt();
System.out.println("Enter passenger's name");
name = sc.nextLine();
System.out.println("Enter number of kms travelled");
km = sc.nextInt();
}
public void calculate()
{
int Rate =0;
if (km <= 1)
  fare = 25.0 * km;
else if(1 < km && km <= 6)
  fare = 10.0 * km;
else if(6 < km && km <= 12)
  fare = 15.0 * km;
else if(12 < km && km <= 18)
  fare = 20.0 * km;
else
  fare = 25.0 * km;
}
public void display()
{
System.out.println("Taxino "+"Name "+" kilometers travelled "+"Bill
amount ");
System.out.println(taxino+ ""+name+" "+" "+fare);
}
public void main()
{
taximeter obj = new taximeter();
obj.input();
obj.calculate();
obj.display();
}//end of main
}//end of class
```

Answer 5

```java
import java.util.*;
class abc
 {
  public void main()
   {
    Scanner sc = new Scanner(System.in);
    double sum = 0.0;
    System.out.println("Input 1 for sum first series and input 2 for
    sum of second series");
    int a = sc.next.Int();
    switch(a)
     {
      case 1:
       {
        System.out.println("Input N value for for the series");
        int n = sc.next.Int();
        for(int i = 1; i<= n;i++)
         {
          sum+ = 1.0/(4.0*i);
         }
        System.out.println("sum of 1st series is "+sum);
       }
      break;
      case 2:
       {
        System.out.println("Input N value for for the series");
        int n = sc.next.Int();
        for(int i = 1; i<=n; i++)
         {
          int fact = 1;
          for(int j = 1; j<=i;j++)
```

```
    fact*= j;
    if(i %2 ==1)
    sum+= (double)i/fact;
    else
    sum-= (double)i/fact;
    }
    System.out.println("sum of 2nd series is "+sum);
    }
    break;
    default: System.out.println("not valid choice");
   break;
   } //end of switch
  } // end of main
 } // end of class
```

Answer 6

```
import java.util.*;
class abc
 {
 public static void main()
  {
  Scanner sc = new Scanner(System.in);
  System.out.println("Enter a sentence ");
  String str = sc.nextLine();
  str = str+" ";
  String word = "";
  for(int i = 0; i <=str.length()-1;i++)
   {
   char ch = str.charAt(i);
   if(ch!=' ')
    {
    word = word + ch;
    }
```

```
        else
          {
          System.out.println(word.charAt(0)+".");
          word = "";
          }
        }
    } // end of main
  } // end of class
```

Answer 7

```
import java.util.*;
class abc
  {
  public static void main()
    {
    Scanner sc = new Scanner(System.in);
    int a[] = new int[10];
    System.out.println("Enter 10 numbers:");
    for(int i = 0; i < 10; i++)
    a[i] = sc.nextInt();
    int largest = 0;
    int smallest = 0;
    for (int i = 0; i < 10; i++)
      {
      if(largest < a[i])
      largest = a[i];
      if(smallest > a[i])
      smallest = a[i];
      }
    System.out.println("Largest of number in array is "+largest);
    System.out.println("Smallest of number in array is "+smallest);
    } // end of main
  } // end of class
```

Answer 8

```
import java.util.*;
class prime
  {
  public static void main()
    {
    int sum = 0;
    for(int i = 2; i <=100; i++)
      {
      int mid = i/2;
      int count = 0;
      for (int j = 1; j <=mid; j++)
        {
        if (i%j ==0)
        count++;
        }
      if(1 == count)
      sum+= i;
      }
    System.out.println("sum of all prime numbers is:"+sum);
    }// end of main
  }// end of class
```

Answer 9

```
import java.util.*;
class prime
  {
  public static void main()
    {
    String temp;
    Scanner sc = new Scanner(System.in);
    String a[ ] = new String [10];
    System.out.println("Enter 10 names all in capital letters");
```

```java
for (int i = 0; i < a.length; i++)
a[i] = sc.next();
for(int i = 0; i < a.length; i++)
for(int j = i+1; j < a.length; j++)
  {
   if(a[i].compareTo(a[j])>0)
    {
    temp = a[i];
    a[i] = a[j];
    a[j] = temp;
    }
  }
  for(int i = 0; i < a.length; i++)
  System.out.println(a[i]);
 } // end of main
} // end of class
```

Variable	Data Type	Description
str	String	Input a string
word	String	To extract character from string
ch	char	To store character
a[ ]	int	To store integer array
temp	int	Temporary variable for swapping
count	int	To count the number of factors.
sum	int	To add the sum of prime numbers
n	int	Number to be checked whether its prime or not
largest	int	To store the largest value
smallest	int	To store the smallest value
a[ ]	String	To read all the names in capital letters.
i,j	int	For looping
temp	String	For storing temporarily

SAMPLE PAPER 2

Attempt all questions

Question 1

(a) State one difference between primitive literals float and double.

(b) What is an infinite loop. Write a statement for infinite loop.

(c) Arrange the operators in the order of higher precedence.

   (1)++ (2)&& (3)>= (4)%

(d) What is final variable and static variable?

(e) What is number of bytes char occupies. Write its range also.

Question 2

(a) What is the difference between keyword parse and function valueOf(). Give example of each.

(b) Write a program code to accept a character input and check whether its digit using its ASCII code. Print character using suitable message.

(c) What do you mean by block. Give one example.

(d) State the difference between entry controlled loop and exit controlled loop.

(e) Write two advantages of using function in the program. And explain role of void in declaring functions?

Question 3

(a) What do you mean by function overloading? Explain with example.

(b) What is this keyword? Also discuss the significance of it.

(c) Attempt the following

    (i) State the two features of a constructor.

    (ii) Write a valid java program code to print the following array in matrix form with 2 rows and 2 columns.

    int mat[ ][ ] = { {2,6},{10,20 }};

    (iii) State the total size in bytes of the array a[4] of char data type and p[4] of float data type.

    (iv) String abc = "helloR";

    StringBuffer str = new StringBuffer(abc);

    int num = str.capacity();

    what will variable num stores the value?

    (v) StringBuffer s1 = new StringBuffer("Robot");

    String s2 = s1.reverse();

    System.out.println("s2 = " +s2);

    System.out.println("s1 = " +s1);

(d) Write a java statement for finding and displaying the position of last space in string 'str'.

(e) Which one of the following returns the corresponding primitive data type object from string object?

    (i) Integer

    (ii) readLine()

    (iii) valueOf()

    (iv) endsWith()

(f) What do you mean by Abstraction and information hiding in java?

SECTION B   (60 Marks)

Attempt any four questions from this Section

The answers in this Section should consist of the Programs in either Blue J environment or any program environment with Java as the base. Each program should be written using Variable descriptions/Mnemonic Codes such that the logic of the program is clearly depicted.

Flow-Charts and Algorithms are not required.

Question 4

Write a program to input three sides of a triangle (s1, s2, s3). Using switch case print whether a triangle is Equilateral, Isosceles, Right angled triangle or scalene.

The program should be used with menu and switch-case.

Question 5

Write a program to find the sum of the following series:

$$x + \frac{x^2}{2!} + \frac{x^2}{3!} + \frac{x^4}{4!} + \ldots n\ terms$$

Question 6

A number is said to be NEON number if sum of digits of square of a number is equal to the number itself.

Example:

INPUT N = 9, Output Square: 81 (where 8 + 1 = 9 so 9 is NEON number)

Write a program to find such numbers between 10 and 10000.

Question 7

Write a program to perform binary search on the list of 10 integers entered by user in ascending order to search for an element input by user, if it's found display the element along with its position else display the message "search element not found".

Question 8

Write a program to accept a word and convert into lowercase if it is in uppercase and display the new word by replacing the VOWELS with the character following it.

    ex. Sample intput: VOWEL

          Sample output: vpwfi

Question 9

Write a program in java to print the following output.

```
1 * 2 * 3 * 4 * 5
    1 * 2 * 3 * 4
        1 * 2 * 3
            1 * 2
                1
```

SOLUTION SAMPLE PAPER 2

Answer 1

(a)

Float	Double
Float occupies 4 bytes in memory	Double occupies 8 bytes in memory

(b) An infinite loop occurs when there is no end to the iteration and loop continues to run indefinitely.

E.g. for (; ;)

System.out.println("10");

(c) ++ , % >= , &&

(d) When any variable is declared using final keyword it makes the the value of that variable as constant. It can't be changed throughout the program.

E.g. final int temp = 90;

Static variable are those which can be used only by static methods. It has only single copy throughout the class.

(e) 2 bytes and its range is 0 to 65,536

Answer 2

(a)

Parse	ValueOf
It converts a variable from string data type to another. E.g. String a = "12"; int b = Integer.parseInt(a);	It converts only from string to int. E.g. string a = "12"; Int b = Integer.valueOf(a);

(b)
```
class abc
   {
   public void main()
    {
    scanner sc = new scanner(system.in);
    System.out.println("Enter the character to be checked");
    char ch = sc.next().charAt(0);
    if(ch >= 91 && ch <= 97)
    System.out.println("Digit is "+ch);
    else
    System.out.println("Its not a digit");
    }
   }
```

(c) Block is a set of statements in a program.

```
Eg
{
System.out.println("example of block statement ");
System.out.println("End of block statement ");
}
```

(d)

Entry Controlled Loop	Exit Controlled Loop

Here condition is checked before entering the loop.
 	
E.g. while(i<3)
 	
{
 	
//some statements
 	
}
	Here condition is checked after entering the loop. First time entering in the loop is must.
	
	E.g.
	
	{
	
	}while (i<3);

(e) Advantages:

It makes the program divides into multiple modules.

Each module is independent in executing its dedicated task.

It helps in reusability of the code once written.

void makes sure that function doesn't return anything.

Answer 3

(a) Function overloading is called when function with the same name is used multiple times with different arguments.

Example:

```
class abc
  {
  public: area(int a);
  area(int a, int b);
  area(int a, int b, float c);
  }
```

(b) This keyword is used as a reference to created object for calling its methods or member functions.

It differentiates between instance variables from the local variables when they have the same names.

(c) (i) Constructor is function which has the same name as that of class without return type. It is called whenever the object is created for the class.

(ii)
```
for(int i =0;i<=2;i++)
{
for(int j =0;j<=2;j++)
System.out.print(mat[i][j]);
System.out.println();
}
```

(iii) char a[4] it occupies 8 bytes.

float p[4] it occupies 16 bytes.

(iv) 22

(v) toboR

toboR

(d)
```
String str = "Blank ";
int a = str.lastIndexOf(' ');
System.out.println(a +" is the last position of ");
```

(e) (i) int

(ii) String

(iii) int

(iv) boolean

(f) Data abstraction is the act of representing the essential features of the program without involving in its complexity.

Information hiding in java means data members which can't be accessed directly by objects instead it has access via its member functions.

SECTION B   (60 Marks)

Answer 4

```java
import java.util.*;
class Triangle
 {
  public static void main()
   {
   Scanner sc = new Scanner(System.in);
   System.out.println("Enter 3 sides of triangle ");
   double s1 = sc.nextDouble();
   double s2 = sc.nextDouble();
   double s3 = sc.nextDouble();
   char ch ='0';
   double sq1 = s1* s1;
   double sq2 = s2 * s2;
   double sq3 = s3 * s3;
   double sum1 = sq1 + sq2;
   double sum2 = sq2 + sq3;
   double sum3 = sq1 + sq3;
   if(s1 == s2 && s2 == s3 )
   ch = 'E';
   if(s1 == s2 || s2 == s3 || s1 == s3)
   ch = 'I';
   if(sum1 == sq3 || sum2 == sq1 || sum3 == sq2)
   ch = 'R';
   if(s1 != s2 && s2!=s3)
   ch = 'S';
   switch(ch)
     {
     case 'E': System.out.println("Equilateral triangle");
       break;
     case 'I': System.out.println("Isoscless triangle");
       break;
```

```java
      case 'R': System.out.println("Right triangle");
        break;
      case 'S': System.out.println("Scalene triangle");
        break;
      default: break;
      }
    }
}
```

Answer 5

```java
import java.util.*;
class series
 {
  public static void main()
    {
    Scanner sc = new Scanner(System.in);
    System.out.println("Enter a number and number of terms");
    int x = sc.nextInt();
    int n = sc.nextInt();
    int a = 1; int f;
    double sum = 0.0;
    for(int i =1; i<= n; i++)
      {
      f = 1;
      for(int j = 1; j<=i;j++)
      f = f * j;
      sum = sum+(Math.pow(x,a)/f);
      a++;
      }
    System.out.println("sum: "+sum);
    }
 }
```

Answer 6

```
import java.util.*;
class Neon
  {
  public static void main()
    {
    int a = 10;
    for(int i =10;i<=10000; i++)
      {
      int a1 = a; long sq = a1*a1;
      int sum =0;
      while(sq >=0)
        {
        int k = (int)sq % 10;
        sum = sum + k;
        sq = sq/10;
        }
      if(sum == a)
      System.out.println(a);
      a++;
      }
    }
  }
```

Answer 7

```
import java.util.*;
class binsearch
  {
  public static void main()
    {
    Scanner sc = new Scanner(System.in);
    System.out.println("Enter the 10 no.s in ascending order to be put in
    the array");
```

```java
int[ ] a = new int[10];
for(int i = 0; i<10; i++)
a[i] = sc.nextInt();
System.out.println("Enter the no. to be searched in the array");
int n = sc.nextInt();
int start =0,pos=0;
int last =a.length – 1;
int mid = (start + last) / 2;
int found = 0;
while(start <= last)
  {
  if(n == a[mid])
    {
    pos = mid; found = 1; break;
    }
  if(n < a[mid])
  mid = last – 1;
  if(n > a[mid])
  mid = start + 1;
  }
if(found == 1)
System.out.println(n+" found at position "+pos);
else
System.out.println(n+" not found ");
  }
}
```

Answer 8

```java
import java.util.*;
class strlol
  {
  public static void main()
    {
    Scanner sc = new Scanner(System.in);
```

```
System.out.println("Enter a word ");
String str1 = sc.next();
String str = str1.toLowerCase();
String word = " ";
for(int i = 0; i <= str.length()−1; i++)
  {
  char ch = str.charAt(i);
  if (ch != 'a' && ch !='e' && ch != 'i' && ch != 'o' && ch!='u')
  word = word + ch;
  if(ch=='a' || ch == 'e'|| ch == 'i' || ch == 'o' || ch == 'u')
    {
    ch ++;
    word = word + ch;
    }
  }
  System.out.println(word);
 }
}
```

Answer 9

```
import java.util.*;
class pattern
 {
 public static void main()
  {
  for(int i = 5; i>= 1; i−−)
   {
   int a = i−1;
   for(int k = 1; k <= 5−i; k++)
   System.out.print(" ");
   for(int j = 1; j<= i; j++)
    {
    System.out.println(j+" ");
    if(a > 0)
```

```
        System.out.println("*");
        a--;
        }
    System.out.println();
      }
    }
}
```

Variable	Data Type	Description
sq1,sq2,sq3	double	To find squares of each side
ch	char	To store the type of triangle.
x, n	int	Number and number of terms.
f	Int	Factorial storing
sum	double	To store sum of series.
sum	Int	To store sum of digits of neon number.
a[ ]	int	To store integers in ascending order.
n	int	Element to be searched.
start,last mid	int	Positions of index of array
found	int	Flag to check element is found or not.
str1	string	For storing string.
ch	char	To take out each character of string.
word	String	For storing the required string.
a	int	Number of rows.

SAMPLE PAPER 3

Attempt all questions

Question 1

(a) What does the default constructor provided by the compiler do?

(b) Name the operators listed below

   (i) >=

   (ii) −

   (iii) !

   (iv) ?:

(e) Name

   (i) A keyword used to call a package in the program.

   (ii) Any reference data types

(c) Why is an object called an instance of a class?

(d) What are identifiers? Give example of each identifier.

Question 2

(a) What is the function of catch block in exception handling? Where does it appear it in a program?

(b) Find the output:

String a = "Sidharthissmartguy",b= "MathsMarks";
String h = a.substring(2,5);

```
String k = b.substring(8).toUpperCase();
System.out.println(h);
System.out.println(k.equalsIgnoreCase(h));
```

(c) (i) Name the mathematical function which is used to find sine of an angle in radians.

(ii) Name a string function which removes the blank spaces provided in the prefix and suffix of a string.

(d) Name the keyword which will be used to resolve the conflict between method parameter and instance variables/fields. Explain with example.

(e) int y = 10 ;
```
y+ = (++y * (y++ +5));
System.out.println(y);
```
What will be the output of the above code?

Question 3

(a) The arguments of the function given in the function definition are called _____.

(b) Why JVM is required in running Java program. Justify your answer.

(c) Attempt the following

(i) Explain with example the possible loss of precision.

(ii) Explain the term type casting in java. How is it useful?

(iii) State the difference between keyword and reserved word.

(iv) What do you mean by convention and rules in java? Explain the difference between compiler and interpreter.

(v) State the purpose and return data type of the following string functions.

a. indexOf()

b. compareTo().

(d) Explain the use of continue statement in looping in java.

(e) State the output of the code:

```
int m = 10;
int n = 10;
for(int i =1;i<5 ;i++)
m++;-n;
System.out.println("m="+m);
System.out.println("n="+n);
```

(f) What do you understand by Java application and java applet. Explain with example

SECTION B   (60 Marks)

Attempt any four questions from this Section

The answers in this Section should consist of the Programs in either Blue J environment or any program environment with Java as the base. Each program should be written using Variable descriptions/Mnemonic Codes such that the logic of the program is clearly depicted.

Flow-Charts and Algorithms are not required.

Question 4

Digital world announces seasonal discount on the laptops in the given order.

Cost of the laptop	Discount
Rs. 20,000 – Rs. 30,000	10%
Rs. 30,000 – Rs. 40,000	15%
Rs. 40,000 – Rs. 50,000	18%
>= Rs. 50,000	20%

An additional discount of 5% on all types of laptops is given. Sales tax is calculated at 12% on the price after the discounts. Define a class to accept the cost of the laptop and print the amount payable by the customer on purchase (use constructor).

Question 5

Write a program in java to accept 10 integers in an array. Now display only those numbers having complete square root

Sample input: 12, 45, 49, 78 , 64, 77, 81, 99, 45, 33

Sample output: 49, 64, 81

Question 6

Write a function to suppress negative elements of an array to bottom without altering the original sequence i.e if array contains 5, −4, 3, −2, 6, −11, 12, −8, 9 Then the return array will be 5, 3, 6, 12, 9, −4, −2, −11, −8.

Question 7

Write a program to input a sentence. Create a function convert(int n).

where n is an integer value in positive or negative.

This function is used to encode or decode the given by shifting each character of a string the number of times as specified by user.

Ex. input – Sid Bowler

Shift value 3

Output – Vig Erzohu

Question 8

Write a program using menu driven mode to find the value of s, where

$S = 2 + 3 + 4 + 4 + 6 + 8 + 6 + 9 + 12...100$ terms

$S = 2! -4! +6! -8!......n$

Question 9

Write a program in java to print the Pascalane triangle as follows.

```
1
1 1
1 2 1
1 3 3 1
1 4 6 4 1
```

SOLUTION SAMPLE PAPER 3

                                      (40 Marks)

Answer 1

(a) Default constructor is helpful in creation of objects of the class.

E.g. ABC obj = new ABC();

(b) (i) Greater than

(ii) predecrement

(iii) logical not

(iv) Ternary operator.

(c) (i) import

(ii) class and arrays

(d) An object is called instance of class because object gets the copy of all variables defined in the class.

(e) Identifiers are the variables, methods classes etc. which are not independent keywords.

E.g. int a;

a is identifier.

Answer 2

(a) The catch block is used to find an exception and handle it. It appears after try block.

(b) dha

false

(c) (i) math.sin()

(ii) trim()

(d) this eg. void assign(int a)

```
{
    this.b = a;
}
```

(e) 186

Answer 3

(a) formal parameter

(b) The JVM converts the Java program into machine code. The computer reads it and displays the output accordingly.

(c) (i) float h = 3.45;
int k = (int)h;

Here k value assigned is 3.

When higher size data type is assigned to the lower size data type there is loss of data which takes place. It's called loss of precision.

(ii) Type conversion is method by which one type of data is converted into other type. It's useful in the expression when calculation is to be done in float type.

(iii) keywords are all reserved words in java example null, true, false are reserved words.

Keywords are like return, continue, break etc.

(iv) Rules are for naming the identifiers. Example identifier name must begin with alphabet or underscore. No special character to be part of the name. Convention is the use the letter of the alphabet.

Compiler compiles the program at once and displays the error for whole program.

Interpreter compiles the program line by line whenever it finds error it stops. At any time it can show only one error.

(v) An application is the program executed on the computer independently. Applet is small program uses another application program for its execution.

(vi) The continue statement makes the next iteration of the loop to be executed.

(vii) a. int – return the index of a character

b. int – compares two strings.

(viii) 11 9

SECTION B   (60 Marks)

Answer 4

```java
import java.util.*;
class dw
  {
  double lc, rate, st1, dst;
  public dw()
    {
    double lc = 0.0;
    double rate = 0.0;
    double st1 = 0.0;
    double dst = 0.0;
    }
  public static void main()
    {
    dw obj = new dw();
    Scanner sc = new Scanner(System.in);
    System.out.println("Enter the cost of laptop");
    obj.lc = sc.nextDouble();
    double ds = 5;
    double fa = 0.0, fa1 = 0;
    if(obj.lc >=20000 && obj.lc < 30000)
```

```java
        {
        obj.rate = 10 ;
        }
     else if(obj.lc >= 30000 && obj.lc < 40000)
        {
        obj.rate = 15;
        }
     else if(obj.lc >= 40000 && obj.lc < 50000)
        {
        obj.rate = 18;
        }
     else if (obj.lc >= 50000)
        {
        obj.rate = 20;
        }
     else
        {
        System.out.println("invalid");
        }
     fa = obj.lc–(obj.lc*(obj.rate + ds)/100);
     fa1 = fa + ((12.0/100.0)*fa);
     System.out.println("Amount payable:"+fa1);
        }
  }
```

Answer 5

```java
import java.util.*;
class lol
  {
  public static void main()
     {
     Scanner sc = new Scanner(System.in);
     int a[ ] = new int[10];
     System.out.println("Enter 10 integers:");
```

```
for(int i =0;i <a.length; i++)
  {
  a[i] = sc.nextInt();
  }
for(int j = 0 ; j<a.length; j++)
  {
  for(int k=0; k<=a[j]/2; k++)
    {
    if(k*k == a[j])
    System.out.println(a[j]);
    }
  }
}
}
```

Answer 6

```
import java.util.*;
class lol
  {
  public static void supress()
    {
    Scanner sc = new Scanner(System.in);
    int a[ ] = new int[10];
    int temp;
    System.out.println("Enter 10 integers:");
    for(int i =0;i <a.length; i++)
      {
      a[i] = sc.nextInt();
      }
    for(int j = 0; j<a.length; j++)
      {
      for(int k=0; k<a.length−1−j; k++)
        {
        if(a[k]<0 && a[k+1]>0)
```

```
        {
          temp = a[k];
          a[k] = a[k+1];
          a[k+1] = temp;
        }
      System.out.println(a[j]);
      }
    }
  }
}
```

Answer 7

```
import java.util.*;
class lol
 {
 public static void convert()
   {
   Scanner sc = new Scanner(System.in);
   System.out.println("Enter a sentence:");
   String str = sc.nextLine();
   String word = "";
   int n = 3; //shift value
   for(int i =0;i <str.length(); i++)
     {
     char ch = str.charAt(i);
     if(ch != ' ')
     word = word + (ch + n);
     else
     word = word + ch;
     }
   System.out.println(word);
   }
 }
```

Answer 8

```java
import java.util.*;
class lol
 {
  public static void main()
   {
   Scanner sc = new Scanner(System.in);
   double sum = 0;
   System.out.println("Enter 1 for number addition and 2 for factorial summation");
   int ch = sc.nextInt();
   switch(ch)
    {
case '1': int a = 2, b = 3, c = 4;
    for(int i = 3; i<=99; i+=3)
     {
     sum = sum + a + b + c;
     a = a + 2;
     b = b + 3;
     c = c + 4;
     }
    sum+=a;
    System.out.println(sum);
     break;
case '2' : int k = 2;
     System.out.println("Enter number of terms:");
     int n = sc.nextInt();
     for(int i = 1;i<=n;i++)
      {
      int fact = 1;
      for(int j = 1; j<=k; j++)
       {
       fact = fact*j;
       }
```

```java
        if(i%2 == 0)
        sum = sum - fact;
        else
        sum = sum + fact;
        k = k + 2;
        }
      System.out.println(sum);
      break;
      default: System.out.println("Error");
      break;
      }
   }//end of main
  }//end of class
```

Answer 9

```java
import java.util.*;
class lol
 {
 static int fact(int n)
   {
   int fact=1;
   for(int i = 1; i <=n; i++)
    {
    fact*=i;
    }
   return fact;
   }
 static int ncr(int n,int r)
   {
   return fact(n) / (fact(n-r) * fact(r) );
   }
 public static void main(String args[ ])
   {
   System.out.println();
```

```
int n, i, j;
n = 4;
for(i = 0; i <= n; i++)
  {
  for(j = 0; j <= n-i; j++)
    {
    System.out.print(" ");
    }
  for(j = 0; j <= i; j++)
    {
    System.out.print(" "+ncr(i, j));
    }
  System.out.println();
  }
}
```

Variable	Data Type	Description
ds	double	Additional discount
fa1	double	Amount payable
a[ ]	int	Array of 10 integers
i,j,k	int	For looping
temp	int	For swapping the numbers
str	String	store the word
ch	char	store character
word	String	store new changed string
sum	double	store sum of series
a b c	int	store consecutive integers.
k	int	store the multiples of 2
fact	int	Store the factorial.

SAMPLE PAPER 4

Attempt all questions

Question 1

(a) What is encapsulation? How does Java achieve encapsulation?

(b) True or False:

   (i) The default case is compulsory in the switch case statement

   (ii) The default initial value of a boolean variable data type is false.

(c) Define the term byte code.

(d) What is the result code stored in x, after evaluating the following expression:

int x = 5;
x+ =++*2+3*−−x;

(e) What is function prototype? Write a function prototype of:

A function poschar which takes a string argument and a character argument and returns an integer value.

Question 2

(a) Show how the sequence {10,5,8,12,45,1,9,11,2,23} changes step by step during the first two passes while arranging in ascending order using the bubble sort technique.

(b) How will you import a scanner package? What is the default delimiter of an instance of the scanner class?

(c) Differentiate between Character. isUpperCase( ) and Character. to UpperCase( )

(d) Write a Java expression: $T = 2\pi\sqrt{L/g}$

(e) What is fall through? Give example.

Question 3

Write the output of the following print statement:

(a) System.out.print ("IXIXI",replace('X '"C').indexOf('C').indexOf('C',2));

(b) System.out.print("robotics".substring(1,3).concat("subject".substring(3)));

(c) System.out.print("FUN WORLD".startsWith("FUN")==

("COMPUTER IS FUN".endsWith("FUN")));

(d) System.out.print(Math.sqrt(Math.abs(Math.ceil(−25.25))));

(e) System.out.print(Math.max(Math.pow(Math.round(6.25),2),(Math.pow(Math.rint(1.8),3))));

Question 4

Write the output of the following segment of code:

a.	String x = "abyz" Int i; for(i=0; i<4; i++) System.out.println(x.charAt(i) − 32);
b.	Int a = 0, b = 10, c = 20, d = 0; a=(b>1)? c >1||d>1? 100:200:300 System.out.print(a);
c.	int m [ ] = {1,4,9,16,25}; int a[ ] = {11}; for(int i = 0;i<5;i++) System.out.println(a[0] + m[i]);

d.	`for(int j = 16;j< = 25; j+ = 2` `System.out.println(j + " " + j–1);`

e.	`int m= 1, n= 0;`
	`for( ; m+n<19 ++n)`
	`{`
	`System.out.println("Hello");`
	`m=m+10;`
	`}`

SECTION B   (60 Marks)

Attempt any four questions from this Section

The answers in this Section should consist of the Programs in either Blue J environment or any program environment with Java as the base. Each program should be written using Variable descriptions/Mnemonic Codes such that the logic of the program is clearly depicted.

Flow-Charts and Algorithms are not required.

Question 5

Given below is hypothetical table showing rates of Income Tax for male citizens below the age of 65 years:

Taxable Income (TI) in Rs.	Income Tax in Rs.
Does not exceed 1,60,000	NIL
Is greater than 1,60,000 and less than or equal to 5,00,000	10% of the amount exceeding 1,60,000
Is greater than 5,00,000 and less than or equal to 8,00,000	20% of the amount exceeding 5,00,000 + 34000
Is greater than 8,00,000	30% of the amount exceeding 8,00,000 + 94000

Write a program to input the age, gender(male or female) and Taxable Income of the person. If the age is more than 65 years or the gender is female, display "wrong category". If the age is less than or equal to 65 years and the gender is male, compute and display the Income Tax payable as per the table given above. Also if Income Tax calculated in over Rs.10,000/- then extra surcharge payable is 2% of the income tax.

Question 6

Define a class Customer described as below:

Data members/instance variables:

String card_holder: Name of the card holder.

long card_holder: card Number

char card_type: type of card (Silver (S) / Gold (G) / Platinum (P))

double amt: purchase made using the card.

Member methods:

(i) Customer( ): Default constructor to initialize all the date members

(ii) void input( ): To accept the details of the card holder

(iii) void compute( ): To compute the cash back after availing the discount of a specific card type as per the following:

Card Type	Cash Back
Silver (S)	2% of purchase amount
Gold (G)	5% of purchase amount
Platinum (P)	8% of purchase amount

(iv) void display( ): To display the details in the format:

Card Holder	Card Number	Card Type	Purchase Amount	Cash Back
XXX	XXX	XXX	XXX	XXX

Write a main method to create an object of the class and call the above member methods.

Question 7

Accept a sentence and print a new sentence with all the odd placed words in uppercase and even placed words in lower case.

Sample input: It is a beautiful world

Sample output: IT is A beautiful WORLD

Question 8

Using switch statement, write a menu driven program to

(i) Accept a number and find a sum of all the even numbers in the number.

Sample input: 24567

Sample output: Sum = 12 (2+4+6)

(ii) Accept a number and print those digits which are divisible by 3

Sample input: 135689

Sample output: Numbers divisible by 3 are 3, 6, 9

Question 9

Write a program to accept 50 student names and their school in two separate single dimension arrays. Search for the school name input by the user in the list. If found, display "Search Successful" and print the name of the school along with the student name, or else display the message "Search Unsuccessful."

Question 10

Design a class to overload a function pattern( ) as follows:

(i) void pattern(int n): with one int argument that prints the pattern as follows:

Input value of n = 5

Output

5

4 5

3 4 5

2 3 4 5

1 2 3 4 5

(ii) void pattern (int n, char ch): with one int argument and one character argument to print the pattern as follows:

Input value of n = 5

Input value of ch = '*'

Output:

1*

1* 2*

1* 2* 3*

1* 2* 3* 4*

1* 2* 3* 4* 5*

SOLUTION SAMPLE PAPER 4

SECTION A   (40 Marks)

Answer 1

(a) Encapsulation is the wrapping of the data and its associated functions into a single unit. Java achieve encapsulation by enclosing the data and methods in the class.

(b) (i) False

   (ii) false

(c) High level program is compiled by java compiler to put in language called bytecode. This is understood by JVM in executing it.

(d) 30

(e) Function prototype is the declaration of function with its return type and number of arguments and data type of arguments.

   int PosChar(String str, char ch);

Answer 2

(a) 10,5,8,12,45,1,9,11,2,23

   5,10,8,12,45,1,9,11,2,23

   5,8,10,12,45,1,9,11,2,23

(b) import java.util.*; Default delimiter for scanner class is white space or tab or newline.

(c) Character.IsUpperCase() checks the uppercase character and returns boolean value.

   Character.toUpperCase() converts lower case character to upper case character and returns upper case character.

(d) doube T = 2*3.14 * Math.sqrt(l/g);

(e) Fall through is a way in which all the cases of switch statement will be executed one by one if break is not encountered.

E.g. After case B is executed it executes case C to F.

```
switch(grade)
 {
 case 'A' :
 System.out.println("Excellent!");
 break;
 case 'B' :
 case 'C' :
 System.out.println("Well done");
 case 'D' :
 System.out.println("You passed");
 case 'F' :
 System.out.println("Better try again");
 break;
 default:
 System.out.println("Invalid grade");
 }
```

Answer 3

(a) 3

(b) object

(c) true

(d) 5.0

(e) 36

Answer 4

(a) 65

66

89

90

(b) 100

(c) 12

15

20

27

36

(d) 16 15

18 17

20 19

22 21

24 23

(e) Hello

Hello

SECTION B   (60 Marks)

Answer 5

```java
import java.util.*;
class Incometax
  {
  public static void main()
    {
    Scanner sc = new Scanner(System.in);
    System.out.print("Enter your gender m or f: ");
    char ch = sc.next().charAt(0);
    if(ch=='f'||ch=='F')
      {
      System.out.println("Wrong Category");
      }
    else if(ch=='m'||ch=='M')
```

```java
{
System.out.print("Enter your age: ");
int age = sc.nextInt();
if(age>65)
  {
  System.out.println("Wrong Category");
  }
else
  {
  System.out.print("Enter your income: ");
  double inc = sc.nextDouble();
  double tax;
  if(inc<=160000)
    {
    tax=0;
    }
  else if((inc>160000)&&(inc<=500000))
    {
    tax = (inc−160000)*0.1;
    }
  else if((inc>500000)&&(inc<=800000))
    {
    tax = (inc−500000)*0.2;
    tax += 34000;
    }
  else
    {
    tax = (inc−800000)*0.3;
    tax += 94000;
    }
  if(tax > 10000)
  tax+= tax* 0.02;
  System.out.println("\nIncome Tax is INR "+tax);
  }
}
```

```
    else
      {
      System.out.println("Invalid Gender");
      }
    }//end of main
  }//end of class
```

Answer 6

```java
import java.util.Scanner;
class Customer
  {
  String card_holder;
  long card_no;
  char card_type;
  double amt;
  double cash_back;
  public Customer()
    {
    card_holder="";
    card_no =0;
    card_type =' ';
    amt = 0.0;
    }
  public void input()
    {
    Scanner scanner = new Scanner(System.in);
    System.out.print("Enter customer name: ");
    card_holder = scanner.next();
    System.out.print("Enter card number: ");
    card_no = scanner.nextInt();
    System.out.print("Enter type of the card [S/G/P: ");
    card_type = scanner.next().charAt(0);
    System.out.print("Enter amount of purchase made using the card: ");
    amt = scanner.nextDouble();
    }
```

```java
public void compute()
  {
  if (card_type == 'S')
    {
    cash_back = amt * 0.02;
    }
  else if (card_type == 'G')
    {
    cash_back = amt * 0.05;
    }
  else if (card_type == 'P')
    {
    cash_back = amt * 0.08;
    }
  else
    {
    System.out.print("Invalid card type ");
    }
  }
public void display()
  {
  System.out.println("Card Holder. \tCard Number. \t Card type \t
  Purchase Amount \t Cash back");
  System.out.println(card_holder + "\t" + card_no + "\t" + card_type +
  "\t" + amt);
  }
public void main()
  {
  Customer c1 = new Customer();
  c1.input();
  c1.compute();
  c1.display();
  }
}
```

Answer 7

```java
import java.util.*;
class lol
 {
  public static void main()
   {
   Scanner sc = new Scanner(System.in);
   System.out.println("Enter a string:");
   String str = sc.nextLine();
   String str1 = str.toLowerCase();
   str1+= " ";
   String word = " ";
   int count = 0;
   for(int i =0; i < str1.length();i++)
    {
    char ch = str1.charAt(i);
    if(ch!=' ')
     {
     word+=ch;
     }
    else
     {
     count++;
     if (count %2 != 0)
      {
      System.out.print(word.toUpperCase()+" ");
      }
     else
     System.out.print(word+" ");
     word ="";
     }
    }
   }
 }
```

Answer 8

```java
import java.util.*;
class lol
  {
  public static void main()
    {
    Scanner sc = new Scanner(System.in);
    double sum = 0;
    int b =0;
    System.out.println("Enter 1 for even number addition and 2 for printing numbers divisible by 3");
    int ch = sc.nextInt();
    switch(ch)
      {
case '1': int a = sc.nextInt();
    b =a;
    while(b % 10 !=0)
      {
      int temp = b %10;
      if (temp %2 == 0)
      sum+=temp;
      b = b/10;
      }
    System.out.println(sum);
    break;
case '2': int k = sc.nextInt();
    b =k;
    while(b %10 !=0)
      {
      int temp = b %10;
      if (temp %3 == 0)
      System.out.println(temp);
      b = b/10;
      }
    break;
```

```
    default: System.out.println("Error");
    break;
    }
  }//end of main
 }//end of class
```

Answer 9

```
import java.util.*;
class lol
  {
  public static void main() {
  String[ ] student_name = new String[50];
  String[ ] school_name = new String[50];
  Scanner sc = new Scanner(System.in);
  for(int i = 0; i < 50; i++)
    {
    System.out.println("Enter students name :");
    student_name[i] = sc.nextLine();
    System.out.println("Enter schools name :");
    school_name[i] = sc.nextLine();
    }
  System.out.println("Enter schools name you want to search:");
  String str = sc.nextLine();
  int flag =0;
  for(int i =0; i < 50;i++)
    {
    if(school_name[i].compareTo(str)==0)
      {
      System.out.println("Search successful ");
      System.out.println(school_name[i]+""+student_name[i]);
      flag = 1;
      break;
      }
    }
```

```java
    if (flag == 0)
    System.out.println("Search Unsuccessful ");
    }
  }
```

Answer 9

```java
import java.util.*;
public class Main
 {
  public void pattern(int n)
   {
    for(int i = n; i>0; i--)
     {
      for(int j = i; j<=n; j++)
      System.out.print(j+" ");
      System.out.println();
     }
   }
  public void pattern(int n, char ch)
   {
    for(int i = 1; i<n; i++)
     {
      for(int j = 1; j<=i*2; j++)
       {
        if(j %2 == 0)
        System.out.print(ch);
        else
        System.out.print("1");
       }
      System.out.println();
     }
   }
  public static void main(String[] args)
```

```
{
System.out.println("Enter the value of n");
Scanner sc = new Scanner(System.in);
int n = sc.nextInt();
System.out.println("Enter the character");
char ch = sc.next().charAt(0);
Main ob = new Main();
ob.pattern(n);
ob.pattern(n,ch);
}//end of main
}//end of class
```

Variable	Data Type	Description
ch	char	For storing character m or f
age	int	Age of person
inc	double	Income of person
tax	double	Store tax
cash_back	double	To store the cashback
c1	Customer	Object of class customer
str	String	To store line or sentence
count	int	Store number of words
sum	double	Store the sum of series
a,b,k	Int	Get the number.
student_name, school_name	String	Array to store student name and school name
flag	int	To know name exists or not
i j	int	For looping
n	int	Number of times to be printed
ch	char	Storing character
ob	Main	Object of class Main

SAMPLE PAPER 5

SECTION A   **(40 Marks)**

Attempt all questions

Question 1

(a) What is the use of 'this' keyword in parameterized constructor?

(b) State the differences between static and dynamic initialization.

(c) What is local variable and global variable? Explain with example.

(d) Which is not keyword in Java:

   (i) boolean

   (ii) void

   (iii) public

(e) int a [ ]; int b [ ] = new int [100]; what is the difference between two initialization.

Question 2

(a) State difference between constructor and method of class.

(b) char ch[ ] = {'a', 'b', 'c', 'd'};
System.out.println("hello world"+ch);

What will be the output of the above code?

(c) Define Java byte code.

(d) State the difference between operator and expression.

(e) What parse function does? Explain with example.

Question 3

(a) What is the use of keyword in void in function declaration.

(b) Which OOP principle is used in function overloading?

(c) Attempt the following:

   (i) Name string function which compares two strings and returns boolean value

   (ii) Write Java statement to do the reverse loop from 19 to 0.

   (iii) Define Java token.

   (iv) What's the value of y after execution.

```
Int y = 5 ;
y −− = ++y + ++y + ++y *3;
```

   (v) int a [ ] = { 'a', 'b', 'c', 'A', 'B', 'C', 'D', 'E'};

```
System.out.println ( (int) a[3]);
System.out.println (a.length);
System.out.println (a[4]);
```

What will the output of the above code?

(d) Write output

```
int i = 20
for(; I<=30; i+=4)
System.out.print(i);
System.out.println(i)
```

(e) Name the formal and actual parameter.

(f) What is the difference between next ( ) and nextLine ( )?

SECTION B   (60 Marks)

Attempt any four questions from this Section

The answers in this Section should consist of the Programs in either Blue J environment or any program environment with Java as the base. Each program should be written using Variable descriptions/Mnemonic Codes such that the logic of the program is clearly depicted.

Flow-Charts and Algorithms are not required.

Question 4

Define a class salary described as below:

Data Members: Name, Address, Phone, Subject Specialization, Monthly Salary, Income Tax

Member methods:

(i) To accept the details of a teacher including the monthly salary.

(ii) To display the details of the teacher.

(iii) To compute the annual income tax as 5% of the annual salary above

rs.1,75,000/-

Write the main method to create object of the class and call the above member method.

Question 5

Write a program to initialize the given data in an array and find the minimum and maximum values along with the sum of the given elements.

Numbers: 2 5 4 1 3

Output: Minimum value:1

Maximum value: 5

Sum of the elements:

Question 6

Define a class to overload following function

double area (double a, double b, double c) $A = \sqrt{s}\ (s-a)\ (s-b)\ (s-c)$

$$S = (a+b+c)/2$$

double area (double x, double y, double h)   area $= 1/2\ h^*\ (x+y)$

double area (double m, double n)   area $= 1/2\ m^*n$

Question 7

Write a program to enter a sentence from the keyboard and count the number of times a particular word occurs in it. Display the frequency of the search word.

Example:

INPUT:

Enter a sentence: the quick brown fox jumps over the lazy dog.

Enter a word to be searched: the

OUTPUT:

Searched word occurs: 2 times.

Question 8

Write a program to create two array names A and B of same size 7. Perform the following operation:

(i) Input in an array A and find square of each number and store in array B and display both array simultaneously.

(ii) Display square root of each number from array A and display square root.

Question 9

Write a program to input a number from user and using binary search method find the number is present in the given array or not. Display proper message.

Array is A [ ] = {24, 39, 330, 343, 763, 789, 909, 1001, 1212, 2000}

SOLUTION SAMPLE PAPER 5

Answer 1

(a) This keyword in parameterized constructor is used to refer to the currently calling object.

(b) Static initialization is used when memory is already allocated and then value is assigned.

Dynamic initialization is used to calculate the value at the run time and then allocate the memory.

E.g. int a = 6,b=9; //static memory allocated.

   int c = a*b; //dynamic memory allocation.

(c) Local variable is a variable whose scope remains inside a method or a block of statements in a java program.

The Global variable is a variable whose scope lies throughout the class in the java program.

(d) boolean

(e) int a[ ] : the array is declared without any allocation of memory space to it.

int b[ ] = new int [100]; The array is declared along with the allocation of memory to it. ie. 400 bytes.

Answer 2

(a)

Constructor	Method
It has same name as that of class.	It has different name than that of class.
It has no return type. It is called when object is created.	It has a return type and is called by the object.

(b) Hello world a b c d

(c) The set of instructions to be executed by the JVM is called java byte code. JVM is the interpreter for java byte code.

(d)

Operator	Expression
It is used to perform an operation.	Set of operators used to perform multiple function.
int a =1, b =2; int c = a+b;	int a =1; a+ = (a++)– ++a + ––a;

(e) Parse function converts the value of a primitive data to the value of another primitive data type.

E.g.: String a = "24";
        int a = Integer.parseInt(a);

Answer 3

(a) The keyword void is used to tell that function has no return type.

(b) Polymorphism.

(c) (i) equals()

    (ii) int i = 19;
        do {
        System.out.println(i);
        i––;
        }while(i>0);

(iii) Java token is the smallest unit of a java program.

(iv) $5 + 6 + 7*3 = 5+6+24 = 32.$

(v) 65

8

66

(vi) 20 24 28 32

(vii) Formal parameter: When the identifier used in function definition to accept the values from the calling function is called the formal parameter.

Actual parameter: when the function is called by passing the identifiers which has values are called as actual parameter.

(viii) next() : it accepts only the word without blank spaces.

nextLine() : It can accept more than one word as well.

SECTION B   (60 Marks)

Answer 4

```
import java.util.*;
class salary
 {
 String name, address;
 String sub;
 double ms, it;
 long ph;
 salary ()
  {
  name = "";
  address = "";
  sub="";
  ms =0.0;
  it = 0.0;
```

```
ph=0;
}
void input ()
{
Scanner sc = new Scanner(System.in);
System.out.println("Enter name address subject monthly salary and
phone number: ");
name = sc.nextLine();
address = sc.nextLine();
sub = sc.nextLine();
ms = sc.nextDouble();
ph = sc.nextLong();
}
void display()
{
System.out.println(" Name: "+name+"\n"+sub+"\n"+"monthly salary:"+ms+
"\n"+"Phone no:"+ph);
}
void calc()
{
if(ms*12<=175000)
it = 0;
else
it = 5.0/100.0 * (ms*12);
ms = ms*12 – it;
}
public static void main()
{
salary oly = new salary();
oly.input();
oly.display();
oly.calc();
}
}
```

Answer 5

```java
import java.util.*;
public class Main
 {
  public static void main(String[ ] args)
   {
   int arr[ ] = new int[10];
   Scanner sc = new Scanner(System.in);
   for(int i =0;i<10;i++)
    {
    System.out.println("enter a number: ");
     arr[i] = sc.nextInt();
    }
   int min = 100000;
   int max = 0;
   int sum = 0;
   for(int i =0;i<10;i++)
    {
    if (arr[i] < min)
    min = arr[i];
    if(arr[i]>max)
    max = arr[i];
    sum+= arr[i];
    }
   System.out.println("Minimum value: "+min);
   System.out.println("Maxmimu value: "+max);
   System.out.println("Sum of elements: "+sum);
   }//end of main
 }//end of class
```

Answer 6

```
import java.util.*;
import java.math.*;
class lol
  {
  double area(double a, double b, double c)
    {
    double s = (a + b + c)/2.0;
    double ar = Math.sqrt(s*(s−a)*(s−b)*(s−c));
    return ar;
    }
  double area(double x,double y,double h,int a)
    {
    double ar1 = 1.0/2.0 *h*(x+y);
    return ar1;
    }
  double area(double m, double n)
    {
    double ar2 = 1.0/2.0*m*n;
    return ar2;
    }
  }
```

Answer 7

```
import java.util.*;
class lol
  {
  public static void process(String a, String str)
    {
    String word ="";
    int count =0 ;
    for(int i =0; i <str.length();i++)
      {
      char ch = str.charAt(i);
```

```
   if(ch!=' ')
   word = word+ch;
   else
     {
     if(a.equals(word))
     count++;
     }
    }//end of for loop
   System.out.println(count);
   }
 }
```

Answer 8

```java
import java.util.*;
import java.math.*;
class lol
 {
  public static void main()
   {
   Scanner sc = new Scanner(System.in);
   int a[ ] = new int [7];
   int b[ ] = new int[7];
   System.out.println("enter a number: ");
   for(int i =0;i <a.length; i++)
     {
     a[i] = sc.nextInt();
     b[i] = a[i]*a[i];
     }
   for(int i =0;i <a.length; i++)
     {
     System.out.println(a[i]+""+b[i]);
     }
```

```
for(int i =0; i<a.length; i++)
  {
  double k= Math.sqrt(a[i]);
  System.out.println(k);
  }
 } //end of main
} //end of class
```

Answer 9

```
import java.util.*;
import java.math.*;
class lol
 {
 public static void main()
  {
  int arr[ ] = {24,39,330,343,763,789,909,1001,1212,2000};
  int first = 0;
  Scanner sc = new Scanner(System.in);
  System.out.println("enter a number: ");
  int key = sc.nextInt();
  int last = arr.length−1;
  int mid = (first + last)/2;
  while(first <= last)
   {
   if (arr[mid] < key)
    {
    first = mid + 1;
    }
   else if (arr[mid] == key)
    {
    System.out.println("Element is found at index: " + mid);
    break;
    }
```

```
    else
    {
    last = mid – 1;
    }
    mid = (first + last)/2;
    }
  if (first > last)
    {
    System.out.println("Element is not found!");
    }
  }//end of main
} //end of class
```

Variable	Data Type	Description
ms	double	Store monthly salary
It	double	Income tax
arr[ ]	int	Store 10 integers
min,max,sum	int	Minimum value maximum value and sum of all elements.
s a b c	double	Semiperimeter lengths of triangle.
ar,ar1,ar2	double	Area of shapes
word	String	Store new word
count	int	Store number of similar words.
a[ ] b[ ]	int	Array of integers and squares
k	double	Square root of number
arr[ ]	int	Static array
key	int	Number to be searched.
first last and mid	int	Indexes of array

SAMPLE PAPER 6

Attempt all questions

Question 1

(a) Define encapsulation.

(b) What are keywords? Give an example.

(c) Name any three library packages.

(d) Name the three types of error, syntax, runtime or logical error in the following case below:

   (i) Math.sqrt (36 − 45)

   (ii) int a;b;c

(c) If int x [ ] = {4,3,7,8,9,10}; what are the values of p and q?

   (i) p = x.length

   (ii) q = x[2] + x[5]*x[1]

Question 2

(a) State the difference between = = operator and equals ( ) method.

(b) What are the type of casting shown by the following examples:

   (i) char c (char)120;

   (ii) int x = 't';

(c) Differentiate between formal parameter and actual parameter.

(d) Write a function prototype of the following:

A function PosChar which takes a string argument and a character argument and returns an integer value.

(e) Name any two types of access specifiers.

Question 3

(a) Define an impure function.

(b) Explain the function overloading with example.

(c) What is default constructor and where is it useful?

(d) State the difference between selection sort and bubble sort.

(e) Int i = 5;
   if (++5/2 = =0)
   System.out.print("EVEN");
   else
   System.out.print("ODD");

(f) Convert the following while loop to the corresponding fir loop:

int m = 5, n =10;
while (n>=1)
{
System.out.println(m*n);
n -- ;
}

(g) Write one difference between primitive data types and composite date types.

(h) Analyze the given program segment and answer the following question:

(i) Write the output of the program segment

(ii) How many times does the body of the loop get executed?

```
for (int m = 5; m<=20; m+=5)
{
if(m%3==0)
break;
else
if (m%5==0)
System.out.println(m);
continue;
}
```

    a. Give the output of the following expression:

       a+=a++ + ++a + --a + a--; when a=7

    b. Write the return type of the following library

       (i) isLetterOrDigit(Char)

       (ii) replace(char, char)

SECTION B   (60 Marks)

Attempt any four questions from this Section

The answers in this Section should consist of the Programs in either Blue J environment or any program environment with Java as the base. Each program should be written using Variable descriptions/Mnemonic Codes such that the logic of the program is clearly depicted.

Flow-Charts and Algorithms are not required.

Question 4

Define a class named BookFair with the following description:

Instance variables/Data members

String Bname – stores the name of the book

double price – stores the price of the book

Member methods

(i) BookFair( ) Default constructor to initialize data members

(ii) void input( ) To input and store the name and the price of the book.

(iii) void calculate( ) To calculate the price after discount. Discount is calculated based of the following criteria

Price	Discount
Less than or equal to rs10000	2% of the price
More than rs1000 and less than or equal to rs3000	10% of the price
More than rs3000	15% of the price

(iv) void display( ) To display the name and price of the book after discount.

Write a main method to create an object of the class and call the above member methods.

Question 5

Using the switch statement, write a menu driven program

(i) To print the Floyd's triangle [Given below]

```
1
2 3
4 5 6
7 8 9 10
11 12 13 14 15
```

(ii) To display the following pattern

```
I
I C
I C S
I C S E
```

For an incorrect option, an appropriate error message should be displayed

Question 6

Special words are those words which starts and ends with the same letter

Example:

EXISTENCE

COMIC

WINDOW

Palindrome words are those words which read the same from left to right and vice versa

Example:

MALYALAM

MADAM

LEVEL

ROTATOR

CIVIC

All palindromes are special words but all words are not palindromes.

Write a program to accept a word check and print whether the word is a palindrome or only a special word

Question 7

Design a class to overload a function SumSeries() as follows:

(i) void SumSeries(int n, double x) – with one integer argument and one double argument to find and display the sum of the series given below:

$$s + \frac{x}{1} - \frac{x}{2} + \frac{x}{3} - \frac{x}{4} + \frac{x}{5} \ldots \ldots \ldots \text{ to } n \text{ terms}$$

(ii) void SumSeries() – To find and display the sum of the following series:

$$s = 1+(1*2)+(1*2*3)+.....+(1*2*3*4*.....n)$$

Question 8

Write a program to accept a number and check and display whether it is a Niven number or not. (Niven number is that number which is divisible by its sum of digits).

Example:

Consider the number 126.

Sum of its digits is $1+2+6 = 9$ and 126 is divisible by 9.

Question 9

Write a program to initialize the seven Wonders of the World along with their locations in two different arrays. Search for a name of the country input by the user. If found, display the name of the country along with its Wonder, otherwise display "Sorry Not Found!".

Seven wonders – CHICHEN ITZA, CHRIST THE REDEEMER, TAJMAHAL, GREAT WALL

OF CHINA, MACHU PICCHU, PETRA, COLOSSEUM

Locations – MEXICO, BRAZIL, INDIA, CHINA, PERU, JORDAN,

ITALY

Example – Country Name: INDIA Output: INDIA – TAJMAHAL

Country Name: USA Output: Sorry Not Found!

SOLUTION SAMPLE PAPER 6

Answer 1

(a) Encapsulation is wrapping up of data and its associated functions into a single unit. It is achieved by the use of access specifiers like public, private, and protected.

(b) Keywords are tokens in java that have a specific meaning.

E.g. static

(c) java.lang

java.io

java.util

(d) (i) logical

(ii) Syntax

(e) (i) 6

(ii) 37

Answer 2

(a)

== operator	equals()
It compares two primitive data types	It compares two strings

(b) (i) Explicit

(ii) Implicit

(c) Formal parameters are used in the function definition using arguments as the input to the function.

Actual parameters are used in calling the above function by passing values.

(d) int PosChar(String str, char ch);

(e) private and protected.

Answer 3

(a) An impure function is a function where the values passed in the formal arguments of function is reflected back in the main function when values are changed by the called function.

(b) void lol()
```
{
String str = "lol";
}
void lol(int a)
{
String str1 = "lol";
}
```

(c) Default constructor is a constructor without any parameter. It is used to initialize class variables to their default values.

(d)

Selection Sort	Bubble Sort
One element is compared with all the elements of the array and position is exchanged at the end of comparison.	Adjacent elements of the array are compared and exchanged.

(e) error

(f) 50

45

40

35

30

25

20

15

10

5

(g) Primitive data type: Its fundamental data types of java.

Composite data type: It's a combination of primitive data type.

(h) (i) 5

10

(ii) 3

(i) 39

(j) (i) boolean

(ii) String

SECTION B   (60 Marks)

Answer 4

```java
import java.util.*;
class BookFair
  {
  String Bname;
  double price;
  BookFair ()
    {
    Bname = "";
    price = 0.0;
    }
```

```java
void input ()
 {
 Scanner sc = new Scanner(System.in);
 System.out.println("Enter name and price of the book: ");
 Bname = sc.nextLine();
 price = sc.nextDouble();
 }
void display()
 {
 System.out.println(" Name: "+Bname+"\n"+"Price:"+price);
 }
void calculate()
 {
 double discount =0;
 if(price <= 1000)
 discount = (2.0/100.0)*price;
 else if(price >1000 && price <= 3000)
 discount = (10.0/100.0)*price;
 else if(price >3000)
 discount = (15.0/100.0)*price;
 else;
 price = price – discount;
 }
public static void main()
 {
 BookFair bf = new BookFair();
 bf.input();
 bf.calculate();
 bf.display();
 }
}
```

Answer 5

```
import java.util.*;
import java.math.*;
class lol
  {
   public static void main(String[ ] args)
    {
    Scanner sc = new Scanner(System.in);
    System.out.println("Enter 1 for number pattern and 2 for string pattern");
    int opt = sc.nextInt();
    switch(opt)
     {
case 1: int a = 1;
     for(int i =1;i<=5;i++)
      {
      for(int j = 1;j<=i;j++)
       {
       System.out.print(a+" ");
       a++;
       }
      System.out.println();
      }
     break;
case 2 : String str = "ICSE";
     for(int i =0;i <str.length();i++)
      {
      for(int j =0;j<=i; j++)
       {
       char ch = str.charAt(j);
       System.out.print(ch+" ");
       }
      System.out.println();
      }
```

```
      break;
      default: System.out.println("ERROR");
     }// end of switch
   }//end of main
 } //end of class
```

Answer 6

```
import java.util.*;
class Main
  {
  public static void main(String [ ]args)
    {
    Scanner sc = new Scanner(System.in);
    System.out.println("Enter a word: ");
    String str = sc.next();
    String word ="";
    for (int i = str.length()-1;i >=0;i--)
      {
      char ch = str.charAt(i);
      word = word+ch;
      }
    if(word.equals(str))
    System.out.println("Palindrome");
    else
      {
      if(str.charAt(0)==str.charAt(str.length()-1))
      System.out.println("special word");
      }
    }
  }
```

Answer 7

```java
import java.util.*;
class lol
  {
  void sumseries(int n, double x)
    {
    double sum =0;
    for(int i =1;i<=n;i++)
      {
      if(i % 2 == 0)
        {
        sum = sum -(x/i);
        }
      else
        {
        sum = sum + (x/i);
        }
      }
    System.out.println("sum = "+sum);
    }
  void sumseries()
    {
    long sum = 0;
    long product = 1;
    for(int i = 1;i <=20;i++)
      {
      product = product * i;
      sum+= product;
      }
    System.out.println("sum = "+sum);
    }
  }
```

Answer 8

```java
import java.util.*;
class lol
  {
  public static void main(String [ ]args)
    {
    Scanner sc = new Scanner("System.in");
    System.out.println("Enter a num: ");
    int a = sc.nextInt();
    int a1 = a;
    int sum =0;
    while(a1!=0)
      {
      int k = a1%10;
      sum = sum+ k;
      a1/=10;
      }
    if(a%sum ==0)
    System.out.println("Niven number");
    else
    System.out.println("Not Niven number");
    }//end of main
  }// end of class
```

Answer 9

```java
import java.util.*;
class lol
 {
 public static void main(String args[ ])
  {
  String wonder[ ]={"CHICHEN ITZA","CHRIST THE REDEEMER", "TAJMAHAL",
  "GREATWALL OF CHINA","MACHU PICCHU","PETRA","COLOSSEUM"};
  String country[ ]={"MEXICO","BRAZIL","INDIA","CHINA","PERU","JORDAN","ITALY"};
  String str;
  int i,len;
  Scanner sc=new Scanner(System.in);
  System.out.println("Enter the name" );
  str=sc.nextLine();
  len=str.length();
  boolean flag=false;
  for (i=0;i<len;i++)
   {
   if(str.equalsIgnoreCase(country[i]))
    {
    System.out.println(country[i]+" "+ wonder[i]);
    flag =true;
    break;
    }
   }
  if(flag== false)
  System.out.println("Sorry Not Found");
  }//end of main
 }//end of class
```

Variable	Data Type	Description
discount	Double	store discount value
opt	int	Option number
i j	int	For looping
a	int	For printing pattern
ch	char	Reading each character of word.
str	String	To read word
word	String	To store reverse word
sum	double	Store the series of sum
product	long	Stores product of integers.
a	int	Read users number
a1	int	Modifying the digits
flag	boolean	To check true or false

SAMPLE PAPER 7

Attempt all questions

Question 1

(a) (i) Name the keyword that makes the variable constant in a program.

(ii) Name the keyword that makes the system to report an error.

    a. Differentiate between equals() and equalsIgnoreCase()

    b. What is the use of access specifier. Name any two.

    c. String s1 = "computer" , s2 ="computers"; System.out. println(s1.compareTo(s2);

    d. Differentiate between linear search and binary search.

Question 2

(a) Write the memory occupied in computer in bytes for array a[5] of character data type.

(b) Differentiate between length() and length functions.

(c) What is error? How logical error differ from syntax error?.

(d) Name the methods of scanner class that:

    (i) Is used to input an integer data from standard input stream.

    (ii) Is used to input a string data from standard input stream.

(e) Write the statement to perform the following task:

   (i) To find and display the position of the first space in the string str

   (ii) To find and display the position of the last space in string str.

Question 3

(a) The arguments of the function given in the function definition are called _____.

(b) Why JVM is required for running java program. Justify your answer.

(c) Attempt the following:

   (i) What is called type casting in java. Explain with example.

   (ii) Write all the possible correct syntaxes of declaring array.

   (iii) What is the purpose of new operator. Why is it useful?.

   (iv) double as =Math.pow("214".indexOf('4',3));

   (v) char a[ ] = {'j','a','v','a'};

```
int c = 1;
System.out.pritnln(a[++c]);
System.out.pritnln(a[c]++);
```

   (vi) Explain the use of return statement in the java.

   (vii) State the purpose and return data type of the following String functions:

      (i) indexOf()

      (ii) compareTo()

   (viii) State the output of the code:

```
int m = 25;
int n = 100;
for(int I = 1; i<5; i++);
m++; --n;
System.out.println("m="+m);
System.out.println("n="+n);
```

SECTION B   (60 Marks)

Attempt any four questions from this Section

The answers in this Section should consist of the Programs in either Blue J environment or any program environment with Java as the base. Each program should be written using Variable descriptions/Mnemonic Codes such that the logic of the program is clearly depicted.

Flow-Charts and Algorithms are not required.

Question 4

Write a program to accept the word from user and print the pattern as shown below:

Sample Input: COMP

Output:

C

CO

COM

COMP

COM

CO

C

Question 5

Write a program to accept the 15 names in the array and arrange them in alphabetical order by bubble sort technique only. And print the output list.

Question 6

Write a program to accept sentence from user and print number of words which starts with vowel and ends with vowel.

Input: india is greatest country

Output: 1

Question 7

Write a program to arrange the words in sentence given by user in alphabetical order. Assume input is in lower case letters only.

Input: india is my country

Output: country india is my

Question 8

Write a program to accept integer values in the array and find the second lowest value from the array without sorting the array.

int a[ ] = {3.10.4,8,12,6,23}

Output: 4

Question 9

Write a function to display the given pattern:

void pattern (int n)

Note: n is the number of rows:

```
1
1 3 2
1 3 5 4 5
1 3 5 7 6 7 8
1 3 5 7 9 8 9 10 11
```

SOLUTION SAMPLE PAPER 7

SECTION A (40 Marks)

Answer 1

(a) (i) final

(ii) throws

(b)

equals()	equalsIgnoreCase()
Compare two strings character by character. Eq: String s1 = "lol", s2 = "lol1"; System.out.print(s1.equals(s2));	Compares two strings ignoring the case of the letters. Eg: String s1 = "lol",s2="lol"; System.out.print(s1.equalsIgnoreCase(s2);

(c) Access specifiers are used to limit the visibility of data according to the users choice.

Eg. private, public.

(d) −1

(e)

Linear Search	Binary Search
One by one search element is compared with all elements of the array.	The array is sorted and then divided into two halves and then search element is compared to the middle element of the array, if its greater than middle element then search is to be done in upper halves and its its lesser than middle element search to be done in lower halves.
The array need not to be sorted.	The array must be sorted.

Answer 2

(a) 10 bytes 24 bytes

(b)

Length()	Length
The method is applicable for finding the length of string.	This is used for finding the array length.

(c) When there is an improper use of statement or statement is logically incorrect then an error is displayed.

Syntax error is displayed when there is improper use of basic java statements.

Logical error is displayed when statement is not giving correct output after execution.

(d) (i) nextInt()

(ii) nextLine() or next()

(c) (i) System.out.println("COMP IS FUN".indexOf(' '));

(ii) System.out.println("COMP IS FUN".lastindexOf(' '));

Answer 3

(a) formal parameters

(b) JVM is used to convert the byte code into machine language which can be run on any machine. In java, the compiler produces machine code for a particular system. Java compiler produces code for a Virtual Machine known as Java Virtual Machine.

(c) (i) The conversion of data from one data type to another datatype is called typecasting.

Eg. char ch = 'A';
Int ch1 = ch;

(ii) int a[ ] = new int [10];
int a[ ];
int a[ ] = {1,2,3};

(iii) The purpose of new operator is to allocate memory to the object. It is helpful in the creation of new object.

(iv) 8.0

(v) (i) v

(ii) a

(vi) It is the keyword in java to return from the method with value or without value.

(vii) (i) Find the index of a character return type is integer.

(ii) Compares two strings return type is integer.

(viii) m=20,n=9

SECTION B   (60 Marks)

Answer 4

```
import java.util.*;
class lol
 {
 public static void main()
  {
  Scanner sc = new Scanner(System.in);
  System.out.println("Enter a word");
  String str = sc.next();
  for(int i =0; i<str.length(); i++)
   {
   for(int j =0; j<=i;j++)
    {
    char ch = str.charAt(i);
    System.out.print(ch+" ");
    }
   System.out.println();
   }
```

```
for(int i = str.length()−2; i<=0; i−−)
 {
 for(int j = 0; j<=i; j−−)
  {
  char ch = str.charAt(j);
  System.out.print(ch+" ");
  }
 System.out.println();
 }
} //end of main
}//end of class
```

Answer 5

```
import java.util.*;
class lol
 {
 public static void main()
  {
  String temp;
  String a[ ] = new String[15];
  Scanner sc = new Scanner(System.in);
  System.out.println("Enter a 15 names");
  for(int i =0; i<a.length; i++)
   {
   a[i] =sc.nextLine();
   }
  for(int i = 0; i<a.length; i++)
   {
   for(int j =0; j<a.length-i-1; j++)
    {
    if(a[j].compareTo(a[j++])>0)
     {
     temp = a[j];
     a[j]=a[j+1];
```

```
      a[j+1] = temp;
      }
    }
  }
  for(int i =0; i<a.length; i++)
  {
  System.out.println(a[i]);
  }
  } //end of main
}//end of class
```

Answer 6

```
import java.util.*;
class lol
  {
  public static void main()
  {
  int count =0;
  Scanner sc = new Scanner(System.in);
  System.out.println("Enter a sentence:");
  String str = sc.nextLine(), word ="";
  for(int i =0; i<str.length(); i++)
    {
    char ch = str.charAt(i);
    if(ch!=' ')
    word = word + ch;
    else
      {
      char ch1=word.charAt(0);
      char ch2 = word.charAt(word.length()-1);
      if((ch1=='a' || ch1=='A' || ch1 == 'e'|| ch1 == 'E' || ch1=='i'||ch1=='I'||
      ch1=='u'||ch1=='U'||ch1=='o'||ch1=='O')&&(ch2=='a' || ch2=='A' || ch2
      == 'e'|| ch2 == 'E' || ch2=='i'||ch2=='I'||ch2=='u'||ch2=='U'||ch2=='o'||
      ch2=='O'))
```

```
      {
        count++;
      }
      word ="";
      }
    }
  System.out.println(count);
  } //end of main
 }//end of class
```

Answer 7

```
import java.util.*;
class lol
 {
 public static void main()
   {
   int count =0;
   Scanner sc = new Scanner(System.in);
   System.out.println("Enter a sentence:");
   String str = sc.nextLine(), word = "";
   str = str+" ";
   for(int i =0; i<str.length(); i++)
     {
     char ch= str.charAt(i);
     if(ch == ' ')
     count++;
     }
   String a[] = new String[count];
   String temp;
   for(int i =0; i<str.length(); i++)
     {
     char ch = str.charAt(i);
     if(ch!=' ')
     word+= ch;
```

```
    else
      {
      int j = 0;
      a[j]=word;
      word = " ";
      j++;
      }
    }
  for(int i =0; i<a.length; i++)
    {
    for(int j =0; j<a.length-i-1; j++)
      {
      if(a[j].compareTo(a[j+1])>0)
        {
        temp = a[i];
        a[j] = a[j+1];
        a[j+1] = temp;
        }
      }
    }
  for(int j =0; j<a.length; j++)
    {
    System.out.print(a[j]+" ");
    }
  } //end of main
 }//end of class:
```

Answer 8

```
import java.util.*;
class lol
  {
  public static void main()
    {
    int count =0;
```

```
int sum = 0;
Scanner sc = new Scanner(System.in);
int a[ ] = new int[10];
System.out.println("Enter 10 values:");
for(int i =0; i<a.length; i++)
  {
  a[i] = sc.nextInt();
  }
int low=0;
int secondlow=low;
for(int i =0; i<a.length; i++)
  {
  if(low >a[i])
    {
    secondlow=low;
    low = a[i];
    }
  }
System.out.println(secondlow);
} //end of main
}//end of class
```

Answer 9

```
import java.util.*;
class lol
 {
 public void pattern(int n)
   {
   int n = 5;
   int l = 0;
   for(int i =1; i<=n; i++)
     {
     int k = 1;
```

```
for(int j = 1; j<=i; j++)
    {
    System.out.print(k+" ");
    k+=2;
    }
int l1 = l;
for(int j = 2; j<=i; j++)
    {
    System.out.print(l1+" ");
    l1++;
    }
l+=2;
System.out.println();
    }
}//end of function pattern
}//end of class
```

Variable	Data type	Description
sc	Scanner	Object for reading data from input stream.
str	String	Store word from user
i,j	int	For looping
ch	char	To reach one character from word.
a[ ]	String	String array for storng 15 names.
temp	String	Storing temporary strings.
count	int	For counting the vowels
word	String	Temporary for storing string
low secondlow	int	Store lowest value and store second lowest value.

SAMPLE PAPER 8

Attempt all questions

Question 1

(a) What is an array. Write the ground syntax for declaring the array.

(b) What is conditional /selection statement in java? Name the operator used for condition checking in java.

(c) What is composite data type. Explain using example.

(d) Which elements of java program represents characteristics and functions of an object.

(e) Define Polymorphism. Which part of the function differentiates between overloaded functions?.

Question 2

(a) What do you mean by function signature in java?

(b) Public static void main() why is main method declared as static?

(c) int i=3; i+=(i++*2)+ −−i*i++ + ++i/2; System.out.println(i); what is the output of the above code?.

(d) Why is the string class called as immutable class.

(e) What's the use of exception handling in java code:

try{ //code here }catch(IO Exception e) {//some code here }what is the use of e.

Question 3

(a) Why is binary search called as divide and conquer.

(b) Differentiate between private and protected access modifiers.

(c) Attempt the following:

(i) Find the output of the following code .

int a=5,b=6,c=9; int g = a>b?a>c?a:c:(b>c)?b:c;

(ii) Differentiate between length and length() function.

(iii) Define class variable vs instance variable

(iv) Write java expression for the following;

$$\frac{\cos x + \sin x}{3.14 * \sqrt{x}}$$

(v) What is the source code in java and what is its extension.

(vi) Write one difference between

(i) char type and String type

(ii) "true" and true.

(vii) State the escape sequence for vertical tab and new line feed.

(viii) Which unit of the class gets called when object is created? Give an example

SECTION B   (60 Marks)

Attempt any four questions from this Section

The answers in this Section should consist of the Programs in either Blue J environment or any program environment with Java as the base. Each program should be written using Variable descriptions/Mnemonic Codes such that the logic of the program is clearly depicted.

Flow-Charts and Algorithms are not required.

Question 4

Write a program to accept the word from user and print the pattern as shown below:

Sample input: COMP

Output:

C
CO
COM
COMP
COM
CO
C

Question 5

Using switch...case write a menu driven program to print

'p' : S
    SS
    ASS
    LASS
    CLASS

'x' :

$$x^1 + \frac{1}{2!}x^2 + \frac{1}{3!}x^3 + ... \frac{1}{n!}x^n$$

Question 6

Write a program to accept sentence from user and print number of words which starts with vowel and ends with vowel.

Input: india is greatest country

Output: 1

Question 7

Write a program to accept a sentence from the user and convert it into uppercase and display the isogram words available in the sentence and also display the count of such words.

(Isogram are words without repetition of the characters)

Input: An important part of life

Output: An part of life

Question 8

Write a program to accept names of 20 students and the total marks scored by them. Arrange the names as per the rank list with maximum marks at the top. Display the final names of the students along with their total marks scored.

Question 9

Write a program to accept a word in upper case and display the position of each alphabet i.e A as 1 B as 2 ...Y as 25 and Z as 26.

Sample Input: CAT

Sample Output: C 3

A 1

T 20

SOLUTION SAMPLE PAPER 8

Answer 1

(a) Array is set of data of the same type.

Eg. int a[ ] = {1,2,3,4,5};

(b) Conditional statements are used to check a condition and print the output accordingly. Ternary operator.

(c) A set of primitive data type is a composite datatype. Eg. Array, Class etc.

(d) Methods and data

(e) The ability to represent a thing in more than one form. The parameters of the function differentiates between the overloaded functions.

Answer 2

(a) Function signature is the part which defines the return type, parameters and visibility of a method.

(b) Main method is declared static because only one copy of the main method is used in the program.

(c) 3 + 6 + 9 + 2 = 20.

(d) String is immutable because once it is stored, it cannot be altered during the execution of the program.

(e) It is used to find the run time errors and catch those errors gracefully. e is object of IO exception class it is used as input to the catch function.

Answer 3

(a) Binary search is called divide and conquer because it divides the array into the equal halves and finds the search element in the lower half and upper half of array accordingly.

(b) Private: accessibility of data or methods is only inside class.

Protected: accessibility of data or methods is only in subclass and package.

(c) (i) 9

(ii) length is used to find the length of array.

Length() is used to find length of string.

(iii)

Class Variable	Instance Variable
Only one copy of these variable is used through out the class.	Multiple copies of these variables are used throughout the class.
Delcared inside the class and outside the methods	Declared inside the methods.

(iv) double x = (Math.cos(x*3.14/180) + Math.sin(x*3.14/180))/(3.14*Math.sqrt(x));

(v) Source code in java is the set of commands in java to be executed by the JVM. Extension is .java.

(vi) (i)

Char Type	String Type
Declared using single quotes ''.	Declared using double quotes" "
Compared by operator ==	Compared by the help of string functions

(ii) "true" → String value

true → boolean value

(vii) "\t" and "\n"

(viii) Constructor

E.g.

```
Class lol
  {
  Int a;
  lol()
    {
    a=10;
    }
  Public static void main()
    {
  lol obj = new lol();
    }
  }
```

SECTION B   (60 Marks)

Answer 4

```
import java.util.*;
class lol
  {
  public static void main()
    {
    Scanner sc = new Scanner(System.in);
    System.out.println("Enter a word");
    String str = sc.next();
    for(int i =0; i<str.length(); i++)
      {
      for(int j =0; j<=i; j++)
        {
        char ch = str.charAt(i);
        System.out.print(ch+" ");
        }
```

```
    System.out.println();
    }
  for(int i = str.length()-2; i<=0; i--)
    {
    for(int j = 0; j<=i; j--)
      {
      char ch = str.charAt(j);
      System.out.print(ch+" ");
      }
    System.out.println();
    }
  } //end of main
 }//end of class
```

Answer 5

```
import java.util.*;
class Main
  {
  public static void main(String[ ] args)
    {
    Scanner sc = new Scanner(System.in);
    System.out.println("Enter p for printing pattern and x for summation
    series");
    char ch = sc.next().charAt(0);
    switch(ch)
      {
      case 'p' : String str ="CLASS";
      for(int i = 0; i<str.length(); i++)
        {
        for(int j =str.length()-1-i; j<str.length(); j++)
          {
          System.out.print(str.charAt(j));
          }
```

```
    System.out.println();
    }
  break;
case 'x': System.out.println("Enter the value of x and n");
    double x = sc.nextDouble();
    int n = sc.nextInt();
    double sum = 0.0;
    for(int i =1; i <=n; i++)
    {
      double fact = 1;
      for(int j = 1; j <=i; j++)
      fact*=j;
      sum=sum+Math.pow(x,i)/fact;
    }
    System.out.println("sum: " +sum);
    break;
    default: System.out.println("Error");
    break;
    }
  }
}
```

Answer 6

```
import java.util.*;
class lol
 {
  public static void main()
   {
   int count =0;
   Scanner sc = new Scanner(System.in);
   System.out.println("Enter a sentence:");
   String str = sc.nextLine(), word ="";
   for(int i =0; i<str.length(); i++)
```

```
  {
  char ch = str.charAt(i);
  if(ch!=' ')
  word = word + ch;
  else
    {
    char ch1=word.charAt(0);
    char ch2 = word.charAt(word.length()-1);
    if((ch1=='a' || ch1=='A' || ch1 == 'e'|| ch1 == 'E' || ch1=='i'||ch1=='I'||
    ch1=='u'||ch1=='U'||ch1=='o'||ch1=='O')&&(ch2=='a' || ch2=='A' || ch2
    == 'e'|| ch2 == 'E' || ch2=='i'||ch2=='I'||ch2=='u'||ch2=='U'||ch2=='o'||
    ch2=='O'))
      {
      count++;
      }
    word ="";
    }
  }
System.out.println(count);
} //end of main
}//end of class
```

Answer 7

```
import java.util.*;
class Main
  {
  public static void main(String [ ]args)
    {
    int count =0;
    Scanner sc = new Scanner(System.in);
    System.out.println("Enter a sentence:");
    String str_ = sc.nextLine(), word ="";
    String str = str_.toUpperCase();
```

```java
for(int i =0; i<str.length(); i++)
  {
  char ch = str.charAt(i);
  if(ch!=' ')
  word = word + ch;
  else
    {
    char [ ]str1= word.toCharArray();
    for(int k = 0; k<str1.length-1; k++)
      {
      for(int j = 0; j<str1.length-k-1; j++)
        {
        if(str1[j]>str1[j+1])
          {
          char temp = str1[j];
          str1[j] = str1[j+1];
          str1[j+1] = temp;
          }
        }
      }
    int flag = 0;
    for(int m =0; m < str1.length-1; i++)
      {
      if(str1[m] == str1[m+1])
        {
        flag = 1;
        break;
        }
      }
    if(flag==0)
      {
      System.out.print(str1+ " ");
      count++;
      }
```

```
    word ="";
    }
   }
  System.out.println(count);
  }//end of main
 }//end of class
```

Answer 8

```
import java.util.*;
class lol
 {
  public static void main()
   {
   String temp; double temp1;
   Scanner sc = new Scanner(System.in);
   String a[ ] = new String[20];
   double b[ ] = new double[20];
   for(int i =0; i<a.length; i++)
    {
    System.out.println("Enter name & marks:");
    a[i] = sc.nextLine();
    b[i] = sc.nextDouble();
    }
   for(int i =0; i<a.length; i++)
    {
    for(int j=0; j<a.length−1−i; j++)
     {
     if(b[j] <b[j+1])
      {
      temp = a[j];
      a[j] = a[j+1];
      a[j+1] = temp;
      temp1 = b[j];
```

```
      b[j] = b[j+1];
      b[j+1] = temp1;
      }
    }
  }
System.out.println("Name " + "\t" + "Marks");
for(int i =0; i<a.length; i++)
System.out.println(a[i]+"\t"+b[i]);
} //end of function main
}//end of class
```

Answer 9

```
import java.util.*;
class lol
 {
  public static void main()
   {
   Scanner sc = new Scanner(System.in);
   System.out.println("Enter a word:");
   String str = sc.next();
   String str1 = str.toUpperCase();
   for(int i =0; i<str.length(); i++)
     {
     char ch = str.charAt(i);
     int a = ch−64;
     System.out.println(ch+"\t"+a);
     }
   }//end of function main
 }//end of class
```

Variable	Data Type	Description
ch	char	For option p or x
str	String	To store "CLASS"
x	double	Variable in the series
sum	double	Stores the sum of series
fact	double	Factorial of number it stores
Str_	String	Stores the word given by user
Str1[ ]	char	String converted into the character array.
temp	char	Temporary storage for character for swapping
flag	int	To check for next consecutive same characters.
m	int	For looping
a[ ]	String	String array to store 20 strings.
b[ ]	double	Array to store 20 marks
str1	String	Store all the capital letter word.
a	int	Store the ascii value of character

SAMPLE PAPER 9

SECTION A   (40 Marks)

Attempt all questions

Question 1

(a) What is return of following function.

  (i) equals()

  (ii) rint().

(b) What do you mean by compound statement. When do you need it.

(c) Explain difference between character constant and string constant.

(d) State any two features of constructor.

(e) Define abstraction.

Question 2

(a) Explain the term object using example?

(b) What is the wrapper class. Justify with example?

(c) State the purpose of new operator?

(d) Write java expression for

$$\sin x + \sqrt[2]{ax^2 + bx + c}$$

(e) Explain the concept of constructor overloading with example.

Question 3

(a) Explain the concept of constructor overloading with example.

(b) Differentiate between equals() and compareTo().

(c) Attempt the following:

(i) Differentiate between call by value and call by reference.

(ii) What is an identifier. Give example

(iii) Name the package that contains the scanner class. Which unit or class gets called when object is created.

(iv) What is meant by encapsulation.

(v) What is meant by inheritance.

(vi) char a[ ]={'a','b','c'}; System.out.println(a); What will be the output.

(vii) char   a[]={'a','b','c'};   System.out.println(a[1]++);   System.out. println(++a[1]);

(viii) int a[ ]={1,2,3}; System.out.println(a[1]++); System.out.println(++a[1]);

SECTION B   (60 Marks)

Attempt any four questions from this Section

The answers in this Section should consist of the Programs in either Blue J environment or any program environment with Java as the base. Each program should be written using Variable descriptions/Mnemonic Codes such that the logic of the program is clearly depicted.

Flow-Charts and Algorithms are not required.

Question 4

Write a program to print the sum of prime digits from given number.

E.g. 134667

Output: 1+3+7=11

Question 5

Write a program to print the longest word from the sentence and print the number of characters of the longest word.

Question 6

Write a program to find sum of negative numbers, sum of positive odd numbers and sum of positive even numbers entered by user and list terminates when user enters 0.

Question 7

Using switch case write a menu driven program to print the patterns.

(a) 0 0 0 0 0
    2 2 2 2
    6 6 6
    12 12
    20

(b) X
    Y Y
    X X X
    Y Y Y Y
    X X X X X

Question 8

Write a program to find using binary search method from list of roll numbers entered by user in ascending order. If the search is successful print " you are selected to go" else print " Try next time".

Question 9

Write a program to input sentence and print in the lowercase letters and replace all the words like "is" and "are" with "were" and "had" and "has" with "had".

SOLUTION SAMPLE PAPER 9

Answer 1

(a) (i) boolean

(ii) double

(b) A set or a block of statement in a program is called compound statement. It can be used to divide the program into segments and organise the data accordingly.

(c)

Character Constant	String Constant
Enclosed in single quotes	Enclosed in double quotes
E.g. 'A', 'e'	E.g. "hello" , "I like JAVA"

(d) It has same name as that of class. It has no return type.

(e) Abstraction is the act of representing the essential features of a program without involving in its complexity.

Answer 2

(a) Object is an identifiable entity with some particular characteristics and behaviour. E.g. TV, characteristics: Big, small etc.

Behaviour: Show different channels, off/on etc.

(b) The class which helps in converting primitive data types to object type is called wrapper class. Eg. Character, Integer etc.

(c) The 'new' keyword supports instantiation. It allocates memory for the newly created object.

(d) double z = Math.sin(x)+Math.sqrt(a*x*x + b*x + c);.

(e) class lol

```
    {
    int a;
    lol()
      {
      a = 1;
      }
    lol(int b)
      {
      a = b
      }
    void main()
      {
      lol obj = new lol();
      lol obj1= new lol(3);
      }
    }.
```

Answer 3

(a) Same as above.

(b)

Equals()	CompareTo()
It returns boolean value	It returns integer value
Compares the whole string at once.	It compares the ASCII values of each character of the string.

(c) (i)

Call by Value	Call by Reference
Actual parameters are copied into the formal parameters.	Actual parameters alias are created in the formal parameters.
Changes made by the formal parameters is not reflected back to the actual parameter	Changes made by the formal parameter directly affects the actual parameters.

(ii) Identifiers are those quantities which change their values during the execution of the program. E.g. Int a, b;

(iii) java.util and constructor.

(iv) Encapsulation: Wrapping of data and its associated functions into a single unit.

(v) Inheritance is the method of inheriting the properties of one class from another class. The class which derives its own properties is called base class and the class which derives the properties of another class is called sub class.

(vi) Address of array a[ ]

(vii) b

d

(viii) 2

SECTION B   (60 Marks)

Answer 4

```java
import java.util.*;
class Main
  {
  public static void main(String[ ] args)
    {
    Scanner sc = new Scanner(System.in);
    System.out.println("enter the number:");
    int a = sc.nextInt();
    int a1 = a; int sum = 0;
    while (a1!=0)
      {
      int count = 0;
      int k = a1%10;
      for(int i=1; i<=k; i++)
```

```
    {
    if(k%i==0) count++;
    }
    if(count==2) sum+=k;
    a1/=10;
    }
  System.out.println("sum = "+sum);
  }//end of main
 }//end of class
```

Answer 5

```
import java.util.*;
class Main
 {
  public static void main(String [ ]args)
   {
   int count = 0; String temp;
   Scanner sc = new Scanner(System.in);
   System.out.println("Enter a sentence:");
   String str = sc.nextLine(), word ="";
   str = str+" ";
   for(int i = 0; i<str.length(); i++)
    {
    char ch = str.charAt(i);
    if(ch==' ')
    count++;
    }
   String a[ ] = new String[count];
   for(int i = 0; i<count;i++)
    {
    for(int j = 0;j< str.length(); j++)
     {
     char ch = str.charAt(j);
```

```
    if(ch!=' ')
    word+=ch;
    else
        {
        a[i] =word;
        word = " ";
        }
    }
}
for(int i = 0;i<a.length; i++)
    {
    for(int j = 0; j<a.length−i−1;j++)
        {
        if(a[j].length() > a[j+1].length())
            {
            temp = a[j];
            a[j]= a[j+1];
            a[j+1]=temp;
            }
        }
    }
System.out.println("LONGEST WORD: "+a[a.length−1]);
System.out.println("No. of characters:"+a[a.length−1].length());
} //end of main
}//end of class
```

Answer 6

```
import java.util.*;
class Main
    {
    public static void main(String[ ] args)
        {
        Scanner sc = new Scanner(System.in);
```

```java
int sum = 0, sum1 = 0, sum2 = 0;
System.out.println("Enter the number to calculate and 0 for exit: ");
int n = sc.nextInt();
int a = n;
while(a!=0)
  {
  if(a>0)
    {
    if(a%2 == 0)
    sum1+=a;
    else
    sum2+=a;
    }
  else
    {
    sum+=a;
    }
  System.out.println("Enter the next number and 0 to exit: ");
  a = sc.nextInt();
  }
System.out.println("Positive even sum: "+sum1+"\t"+"Positive odd
sum:"+sum2+"\t"+"Negative sum:"+sum);
} //end of main
}//end of class
```

Answer 7

```java
import java.util.*;
class Main
  {
  public static void main(String[] args)
    {
    Scanner sc = new Scanner(System.in);
    System.out.println("Enter the choice:");
```

```java
    int a1 = sc.nextInt();
    switch(a1)
     {
case 1:
     int a = 0;
     int b = 2;
     for(int i =5;i>= 1;i--)
      {
      for(int j=1; j<=i;j++)
      System.out.print(a+" ");
      a+=b;
      b+=2;
      System.out.println();
      }
     break;
case 2:
     for(int i =1; i<=5; i++)
      {
      for(int j=1;j<=i; j++)
       {
       if(j%2 != 0)
       System.out.print("X");
       else
       System.out.print("Y");
       }
      System.out.println();
      }
     break;
     default: System.out.println("Invalid Choice");
     }
   } //end of main
  }//end of class
```

Answer 8

```java
import java.util.*;
class Main
  {
  public static void main(String args[ ])
    {
    int first, last, middle, n, search, array[ ];
    Scanner sc = new Scanner(System.in);
    System.out.println("Enter total number of students");
    n = sc.nextInt();
    array = new int[n];
    System.out.println("Enter " + n + " integers");
    for (int i = 0; i<n; i++)
    array[i] = sc.nextInt();
    System.out.println("Enter value to find");
    search = sc.nextInt();
    first = 0;
    last = n – 1;
    middle = (first + last)/2;
    while(first <= last)
      {
      if (array[middle] < search)
      first = middle + 1;
      else if (array[middle] == search)
        {
        System.out.println(search + " you are selected to go " + (middle + 1)
        + ".");
        break;
        }
      else
      last = middle – 1;
      middle = (first + last)/2;
      }
    if (first > last)
    System.out.println(search + " Try next time.\n");
    } //end of main
  } //end of class
```

Answer 9

```
import java.util.*;
class Main
 {
 public static void main(String[ ] args)
  {
  Scanner sc = new Scanner(System.in);
  System.out.println("Enter the sentence:");
  String str = sc.nextLine();
  String str1 = str.toLowerCase();
  String word = "";
  str1+=" ";
  String str2 ="";
  for(int i =0;i<str1.length(); i++)
   {
   char ch = str1.charAt(i);
   if(ch!=' ')
   word+=ch;
   else
    {
    if(word .equals("is"))
    str2=str2+"were"+" ";
    else if(word.equals("are"))
    str2=str2 + "had"+" ";
    else if(word.equals("has"))
    str2=str2+"had" +" ";
    else
    str2=str2+word+" ";
    word = "";
    }
   }
  System.out.println(str2);
  } //end of main
}//end of class
```

Variable	Data Type	Description
a	int	Store input integer from user
a1,sum	int	For modifying digits and to calculate sum of digits
str	String	Store input string from user
ch	char	Store the character
count	int	Count number of blank spaces
word	String	To store new word
temp	String	Temporary storage for swapping strings.
a[ ]	String	Array of strings.
n	int	Store integer from user
a	int	For modifying value
sum1,sum2,sum3	int	Even number sum Positive odd sum Negative sum
b	int	For printing even pattern
i j	int	For looping
first last middle n search array[ ]	int	First last and middle are Index of array N is total number of elements Search is number to be searched in array. Array[ ] array of sorted roll numbers
str1	String	Store lowercase word
str2	String	To store the modified sentence.

SAMPLE PAPER 10

(40 Marks)

Attempt all questions

Question 1

(a) What do you mean by abstraction.

(b) Using an example explain the term object.

(c) What is wrapper class.

(d) State the use of new operator.

(e) Write a java expression for square root of sinx.

Question 2

(a) Differentiate between local variable and global variable.

(b) What is the purpose of default in switch statement?

(c) Define an impure function.

(d) What is called default constructor?

(e) Explain the concept of constructor overloading using an example.

Question 3

(a) How java make use of formal and actual parameter?

(b) State the java concept that is implemented into smaller groups

    (i) Dividing a long set of instruction into smaller groups and modules.

    (ii) Wrapping up of data and its associated function into a class.

(c) Attempt the following:

  (i) What is role of access specifier?

  (ii) Why is java platform independent?

  (iii) Differentiate between public and private visibility label.

  (iv) Int a = 7,b = 6; b = a>b?a!=0?3:b<10?9:4:8; System.out.println(b);

  (v) Int a = 7,b = 6; b=++a+ ++a/ ++a; System.out.println(b);

  (vi) What are functions? Give one advantage of using functions.

  (vii) How do objects communicate with each other?

  (viii) What are two types of methods? Give two concrete differences between them and include example of each type of function from java.lang.Math class.

SECTION B   (60 Marks)

Attempt any four questions from this Section

The answers in this Section should consist of the Programs in either Blue J environment or any program environment with Java as the base. Each program should be written using Variable descriptions/Mnemonic Codes such that the logic of the program is clearly depicted.

  Flow-Charts and Algorithms are not required.

Question 4

A Smith number is a composite number, the sum of whose digits is the sum of the digits of its prime factors obtained as a result of prime factorization(excluding 1).

  The first few such numbers are 4,22,27,58,85,94,121.........

  eg. 666

  Prime factors are 2,3,3 and 37

  Sum of the digits are (6+6+6) = 18

  Sum of the digits of the factors (2+3+3+3+7)=18

  Write a program to input a number and display whether the number is a Smith number or not.

Question 5

Write a program to assign a full path and file name as given below. Using library functions, extract and output the file path, file name and file extension separately as shown.

Input: C:\users\sid\pictures\cricket.jpg

output: C:\users\sid\pictures

File name: Cricket

Extension: jpg

Question 6

Write a program to input a word from user and remove the consecutive repeated characters by replacing the sequence of repeated characters by its single occurrence.

input: ssiiddaarrtth

Output: sidarth

Question 7

Write a program in java to input a number and check whether it is Duck number or not.

Note: A Duck number is a number which has zeroes present in it, but there should be no zero present in the beginning of the number. For example 3210, 7056, 8430709 are all duck numbers whereas 08237,04309 are not.

Question 8

Write a program in java to input a number in Decimal number system and convert it into its equivalent number in the octal number system.

Note: Octal number system is a number system which can represent a number in any other number system in terms of digits ranging from 0 to 7 only. This number system consists of only eight basic digits i.e. 0,1,2,3,4,5,6 and 7.

eg. 25 in the decimal number system can be represented as 31 in the octal number system.

Question 9

Using Scanner class, write a program to input a string and display all those words of the strings which begins with capital letter and end with a small letter.

Sample Input: We all love Java for School Students because of its Uniqueness

Sample Output: We Java School Students Uniqueness

SOLUTION SAMPLE PAPER 10

Answer 1

(a) Abstraction is the act of representing the essential features of the program without involving in its complexity. Eg. While using computer user is not concerned about the different parts of the computer only needs to know about usage.

Characteristics (big, small, flat etc)

(c) Wrapper class is a class which helps to convert a primitive data type to object type. E.g. Integer, Short etc.

(d) New operator supports instantiations. It is used to allocate memory space to the newly created object.

E.g. Scanner sc = new Scanner(System.in)

(e) double d = Math.sin(x*3.14/180);

Answer 2

(a)

Local Variable	Global Variable
Scope remains only inside a block or a function.	Scope remains throughout the class.
Multiple copies of the variable are used throughout the class.	Only a single copy of the variable is used throughout the class.

(b) When none of the cases of the switch statement are satisfied, the default case is used and executed in the program.

(c) An impure function is a function where values of the arguments keep changing during the execution of the program.

(d) A default constructor is a constructor without any parameters. It is used to assign a default value to the class variables.

(e) class lol

```
{
int a; int n;
lol()
  {
  a=0;
  }
lol(int c)
  {
  a=1;
  }
public static void main()
  {
  lol obj = new lol();
  lol obj1=new lol(2);
  }
}
```

Answer 3

(a) Formal parameters are used in the function definition of the program while actual parameters are used in the function call statement.

(b) object oriented programming

Encapsulation

(c) (i) Access specifiers are used to moderate the accessibility of the data according to user's choice.

(ii) Java is platform independent because the JVM can interpret the byte code which can run on any platform.

(iii) Public: It can be accessed anywhere.

Private: It can be accessed only inside the class.

(iv) 3

(v) b=8+9/10=8+0=8

(vi) A function is block of statements in a java program used to perform certain tasks. It organizes the data into segments and helps in performing tasks easily.

(vii) Objects communicate with each other using methods.

(viii)

Pure Function	Impure Function
Functions where the value of variables don't change	Function where the values of the variables changes.
Depends on the actual parameters passed in the function call.	Depends on where created object calls the functions.
E.g. Math.sqrt()	E.g. Math.random(i)

SECTION B   (60 Marks)

Answer 4

```
import java.util.*;
class Main
 {
 int sumDig(int n)
  {
  int sum=0;
  while(n>0)
   {
   sum+=n%10;
   n=n/10;
   }
  return sum;
  }
```

```java
int sumPrimeFact(int n)
 {
 int i=2, sum=0;
 while(n>1)
  {
  if(n%i==0)
   {
   sum=sum+sumDig(i);
   n=n/i;
   }
  else
  i++;
  }
 return sum;
 }
public static void main(String[ ] args)
 {
 Main ob=new Main();
 Scanner sc = new Scanner(System.in);
 System.out.print("Enter a Number: ");
 int n=sc.nextInt();
 int a=ob.sumDig(n);
 int b=ob.sumPrimeFact(n);
 if(a==b)
 System.out.print("It is a Smith Number");
 else
 System.out.print("It is Not a Smith Number");
 }// end of main
}//end of class
```

Answer 5

```
import java.util.*;
class Main
  {
  public static void main(String args[ ])
    {
    Scanner sc = new Scanner(System.in);
    System.out.println("Input the file path:");
    String str = sc.nextLine();
    String str1 = str.substring(0,str.lastIndexOf('\\'));
    String str2 = str.substring(str.lastIndexOf('\\')+1);
    String str3 = str2.substring(str2.indexOf(' ')+1);
    System.out.println("Path:" +str1);
    System.out.println("Filename:"+str2);
    System.out.println("Extension:"+str3);
    }//end of main
  }//end of class
```

Answer 6

```
import java.util.*;
class Main
  {
  public static void main(String args[ ])
    {
    String word = "";
    Scanner sc = new Scanner(System.in);
    System.out.println("Input the sentence:");
    String str = sc.nextLine();
    char chprev=' ';
```

```
for(int i =0;i<str.length();i++)
  {
  char ch = str.charAt(i);
  if(chprev!=ch)
    {
    word+=ch;
    chprev = ch;
    }
  else
  continue;
  }
System.out.println("word without successive repeated characters
is:"+word);
} //end of main
}//end of class
```

Answer 7

```
import java.util.*;
class Main
  {
  public static void main(String args[ ])
    {
    Scanner sc = new Scanner(System.in);
    System.out.println("Input the number:");
    int a = sc.nextInt();
    int a1 = a; int count =0;
    String str = Integer.toString(a);
    while(a1!=0)
      {
      if(str.charAt(0)==0)
      break;
      else
```

```
    {
    int k = a1%10;
    if(k==0) count++;
    a1/=10;
    }
    }
  if(count>=1)
  System.out.println("Duck no.");
  else
  System.out.println("Not Duck no.");
  } //end of main
 }//end of class
```

Answer 8

```
import java.util.*;
class Main
  {
  public static void main(String args[ ])
    {
    Scanner sc = new Scanner(System.in);
    System.out.println("Input the decimal number:");
    int a = sc.nextInt();
    int a1=a%8; int a2 = a/8;
    String str=""; int a3=a2%8;
    String str1 = Integer.toString(a1);
    String str2 = Integer.toString(a3);
    str=str2+str1;
    int ah = Integer.parseInt(str);
    System.out.print(ah);
    } //end of main
 }//end of class
```

Answer 9

```java
import java.util.*;
class Main
 {
  public static void main(String args[ ])
   {
   String word = "";
   Scanner sc = new Scanner(System.in);
   System.out.println("Input the sentence:");
   String str = sc.nextLine();
   str+=" ";
   for(int i =0;i<str.length();i++)
    {
    char ch = str.charAt(i);
    if(ch!=' ')
    word+=ch;
    else
     {
     if(Character.isUpperCase(word.charAt(0))&&Character.isLowerCase(word.
     charAt(word.length()−1)))
      {
      System.out.print(word+" ");
      }
     word = "";
     }
    }
   }//end of main
 }//end of class
```

Variable	Data Type	Description
sum	int	To store sum of digits of number
n	int	Number whose digits are to be added
sum	int	To store sum
i	int	To start with 2
b	int	Store sum of prime factors
a	int	Store sum of digits
str	String	Store the string
str1	String	To store the path
str2	String	To store filename
str3	String	Store file extension
word	String	To store modified word
ch	char	to store character
chprev	char	To store previous character
a a1 count	int	Users input number, modified number and count number of 0
a1	int	To store octal number last digit
a2	int	Quotient after dividing by 8
a3	int	Quotient after dividing by 8
str1	String	To store a1 as string
str2	String	To store a2 as string
ah	int	Store converted integer from string.

SAMPLE PAPER 11

Attempt all questions

Question 1

(a) Give one similarity and one difference between do while and while loop.

(b) Write the java statement to find largest of 3 numbers using conditional operator.

(c) What is polymorphism?

(d) Write a function to round off any fractional number? Give one example.

(e) What is difference between infinite loop and fall through statement?

Question 2

(a) Compare local, instance and class variables on the basis of the given criteria.

   (i) identification in program

   (ii) Usage of access specifier with them.

   (iii) provision of initial values.

   (iv) Number of copies for each object of class.

(b) Which OOPs principle is implemented when you:

   (i) use the keyword extends

   (ii) create an interface

(iii) create various functions

(iv) use private data members?

(c) What are functions? Give one advantage using functions.

(d) Differentiate between classes and objects. Why is object referred as instance of class?

(e) Differentiate between linear search and binary search.

Question 3

(a) What is other name of java interpreter? Explain it.

(b) Name the java keyword

(i) used to finish the execution of the method.

(ii) used to implement the concept of inheritance.

(c) Attempt the following:

(i) Assign the constant value pi as 3.14 to variable using suitable data type?

(ii) Give difference between unary and binary operators.

(iii) Give examples of each

(i) Composite date type.

(ii) Escape sequence.

(iii) Comment lines

(iv) Wrapper class

(iv) Write any two rules of naming variable

(v) Differentiate between type conversion and coericion.

(vi) State the difference between final and finally.

(vii) a. State the use of toString() and valueOf().

b. Write a statement to extract the last word of the string str.

(viii) a. What is called byte code?

b. Explicit and implicit type conversion.

SECTION B   (60 Marks)

Attempt any four questions from this Section

The answers in this Section should consist of the Programs in either Blue J environment or any program environment with Java as the base. Each program should be written using Variable descriptions/Mnemonic Codes such that the logic of the program is clearly depicted.

Flow-Charts and Algorithms are not required.

Question 4

Using switch case write a menu driven program to print the patterns.

(a) 0 0 0 0 0
    2 2 2 2
    6 6 6
    12 12
    20

(b) X
    Y Y
    X X X
    Y Y Y Y
    X X X X X

Question 5

Write a program to print the frequency of the digits occurring in number.

Eg. 2566773

Output: 2 1
         5 1
         6 2
         7 2
         3 1

Question 6

Write a class with a special member function to input a multi digit number(max 9 digit) and print the following:

(i) total number of even and odd digits

(ii) the reverse number

(iii) total number of zeros present.

Question 7

Write a class to input a string (combination of letters and digits) and replace the repeated characters with star(*) sign. Then display both old and newly created string.

Question 8

Write a program to print the following pattern by taking the input n from the user.

Note: n determines number of rows.

Eg. n = 4

Output:

* * * *

* * *

* * * *

* * *

Question 9

Write a java class to calculate and print the electricity bill to be paid by a customer.

Assume that the customer pays a rent of Rs.350.00

No. of units	Charge per unit
Upto 100 units	Rs. 1.50
For the next 100 units	Rs. 2.00
For next 50 units	Rs. 2.50
Beyond 250 units	Rs. 4.00

SOLUTION SAMPLE PAPER 11

Answer 1

(a) Similarity – Both while and do while loop is used when the no. of iterations are not specified.

Difference: while loop is entry controlled loop and while do while loop is exit controlled.

(b) int a = (b>c)?b:c;
    int d = (a>e)?a:e;

(c) Polymorphism is the identity to represent an object in more than one form.

(d) Math.round()
    double k = Math.round(2.9);.

(e)

Infinite Loop	Fall Through
Occurs for iteration statement	Occurs for conditional statement.
Occurs when conditions is always satisfied.	Occurs when the break statement is missing in every case statement.

Answer 2

(a) (i) Local variables are usually used in a block of statement. Instance variables are used by a method while class variable has only one copy throughout out the class.

(ii) Local variable scope remains inside the compound statement. Inside the curly braces.

Instance variable scope remains inside the method. All access specifiers can be used in class variables. Scope is throughout the class.

(iii) Local variables is initialized in its scope.

Instance variables initialized in the method where it is used in.

Class variables are initialized after the class declaration.

(iv) local variables multiple copies can exists.

Instance variables multiple copies can exists.

Class variables single copy exists.

(b) (i) Inheritance

(ii) Abstraction

(iii) Polymorphism

(iv) Encapsulation

(c) Functions are a set of statements used to perform certain tasks. Advantage: It organizes the code into a blocks and helps in performing specific task.

(d) (i) Object is an identifiable entity with some characteristics and behaviour. Class is a collection of object with similar characteristics.

(ii) Object is called instance of class as object helps in accessing the class members and functions to get the required output.

(e)

Linear Search	Binary Search
The search element is compared with each element of the array.	The array is sorted and divided into two halves and then search element is found accordingly.
Array need not be sorted.	Array has to be sorted.

Answer 3

(a) JVM (Java virtual machine): It is used to convert java byte code to machine code which can be understood by the computer running on any operating system.

(b) (i) exit or return

(ii) extends

(c) (i) double const pi =3.14;

(ii) Unary operator is is used for one operand.

Binary operator is used for two operands.

(iii) (i) Array, class

(ii) "\n","\\'

(iii) // or /* java */

(iv) Character, Integer

(iv) Variables should not be keyword and it should not start with digit or special character except for the $ and & and _. It must start with alphabet.

Type conversion	Coercion
Assigning one data type to another	Promotion of data type
It's called implicit type casting	Also called type promotion.

(v) Final makes a variable constant throughout the program. Finally is a block which is always executed even if exception occurred or not.

(vi) a.

toString()	valueOf()
Converts integer to string.	Converts strings to integer.

b. String word = str.substring(sr.lastIndexOf(' ')+1);

(vii) a. Byte code is an specific set of instruction to be executed by the JVM.

b. Implicit type conversion: Java compiler will automatically convert one data type to another when data types are compatible.

E.g. int I = 10;

double b = I;

Explicit type conversion: Java compiler is to be told explicitly to do the conversion form one data type to another. E.g.

double d = 10.0;

float f = (float)d;

SECTION B   (60 Marks)

Answer 4

```
import java.util.*;
class Main
  {
  public static void main(String[ ] args)
    {
    Scanner sc = new Scanner(System.in);
    System.out.println("Enter the choice:");
    int a1 = sc.nextInt();
    switch(a1)
      {
case 1: int a =0;
    int b = 2;
    for(int i =5;i>= 1;i--)
      {
      for(int j=1; j<=i;j++)
      System.out.print(a+" ");
```

```
       a+=b;
       b+=2;
       System.out.println();
       }
     break;
case 2: for(int i =1 ; i<=5; i++)
       {
       for(int j=1;j<=i; j++)
         {
         if(j%2 != 0)
         System.out.print("X");
         else
         System.out.print("Y");
         }
       System.out.println();
       }
     break;
     default: System.out.println("Invalid Choice");
       }
     } //end of main
   }//end of class
```

Answer 5

```
import java.util.*;
class Main
   {
   static int frequency(int number, int digit)
     {
     int count = 0;
     while (number > 0)
       {
       if (number % 10 == digit)
       count++;
```

```
      number = number / 10;
    }
  return count;
  }
 public static void main(String args[ ])
   {
   Scanner sc = new Scanner(System.in);
   System.out.println("Input the number:");
   int n = sc.nextInt();
   int a = n;
   int search = 0;
   int countdigit = 0;
   int [ ]arr = new int[10];
   while(a >0)
     {
     search = a%10;
     countdigit = frequency(n,search);
     if(countdigit>0)
       {
       arr[search]=countdigit;
       countdigit=0;
       }
     a=a/10;
     }
   for(int i =0; i<arr.length;i++)
     {
     if(arr[i]>0)
     System.out.println(i+"\t"+arr[i]);
     }
   } //end of main
 } //end of class
```

Answer 6

```
import java.util.*;
class Main
 {
 public static void main(String args[ ])
  {
  Scanner sc = new Scanner(System.in);
  System.out.println("Input the number:");
  long a = sc.nextInt();
  int sumeven =0;
  int sumodd =0, sum3 = 0;
  String str = "";
  long a1 = a;
  while(a1<=999999999&&a1!=0)
   {
   int k = (int)a1%10;
   str+=Integer.toString(k);
   if(k%2 == 0)
   sumeven++;
   else if(k%2!=0)
   sumodd++;
   else if (k==0)
   sum3++;
   else;
   a1=a1/10;
   }
  System.out.println("No.  even:  "+sumeven+"\t"+  "odd:"+sumodd+"\
  t"+"zero: "+sum3+"\t"+"Reverse no:"+str);
  } //end of main
 } //end of class
```

Answer 7

```java
import java.util.*;
class Main
 {
  public static void main(String[ ] args)
   {
   Scanner sc=new Scanner(System.in);
   System.out.println("Enter a sentence: ");
   String str=sc.nextLine();
   for(int i=0;i<str.length();i++)
    {
    char ch=str.charAt(i);
    if(ch!='*')
     {
     for(int j=str.length()-1;j>i;j--)
      {
      char ch1=str.charAt(j);
      if(ch==ch1)
       {
       StringBuffer str1=new StringBuffer(str);
       str1.setCharAt(j,'*');
       str=""+str1;
       }
      }
     }
    }
   System.out.println(str);
  }//end of main
 }//end of class
```

Answer 8

```java
import java.util.*;
class Main
 {
 public static void main(String args[ ])
   {
   Scanner sc = new Scanner(System.in);
   System.out.println("Input the number:");
   int n = sc.nextInt();
   for(int i = 1; i <=n;i++)
     {
     if(i%2==0)
       {
       for(int j =1; j<=3;j++)
       System.out.print(" *");
       }
     else
       {
       for(int j =1; j<=4;j++)
       System.out.print("* ");
       }
     System.out.println();
     }
   } //end of main
 } //end of class
```

Answer 9

```java
import java.util.*;
class Main
 {
  public static void main(String[ ] args)
   {
   Scanner sc=new Scanner(System.in);
   double fixed_price = 350.0;
   double amt = 0.0;
   System.out.println("Enter a unit of electricity consumption: ");
   int n=sc.nextInt();
   if(n<=100)
   amt+= amt+1.5*n;
   else if(n>100&&n<=200)
   amt+= 100*1.5+(n−100)*2.0;
   else if(n>200&&n<=250)
   amt+= 100*1.5+(100)*2.0 + (n−200)*2.5;
   else
   amt+= 100*1.5+(100)*2.0 + (50)*2.5+(n−250)*4.0;
   System.out.println("Electricity bill amount: "+amt);
   }//end of main
 }//end of class
```

Variable	Data Type	Description
a1	int	Store users choice
a b	int	For printing pattern
i j	int	For looping
number	int	Number in which digits to be searched
digit	int	Digit which is to be searched.
count	int	Counting number of digits
n	int	Users input number
arr[ ]	int	Array of 10 integers.
search, countdigit	int	Digit to be searched and count of that digit
sumeven,sumodd, sum3	int	Sum of even digits, sum of odd digits and count of zero.
str	String	User input string
str1	String Buffer	To store modified string
ch	char	To store character
fixed_price,amt	double	For fixed price and calculating amount

SAMPLE PAPER 12

SECTION A   (40 Marks)

Attempt all questions

Question 1

(a) What do you mean by reusability feature.

(b) Write the java expression for the roots of the quadratic equation.

(c) Name any two jump statments and their usages.

(d) (i) Name the mathematical function which is used to find the cosine of an angle given in radians.

    (ii) Name a string functions which removes the blank spaces provided in the prefix and suffix of a string.

(e) What do you mean by dynamic initialization of an array? Give an example.

Question 2

(a) Consider the following code

```
class lol
 {
 public static int m=3,y=4;
 public int a =10,b = 15;
 }
```

    (i) Name the variables for which each of object of the class will have its own distinct copy.

    (ii) Name the variables that are common to all the objects of the class.

(b) Distinguish between constructor and method.

(c) What are the values of a and b after the following function is executed if values passed are 30 and 50.

```
void pass(int a, int b)
{
a = a+b;
b= a−b;
a = a−b;
System.out.println("a="+a+","b="+b);
}
```

(d) Rewrite the following statement using if-else statement amount = (x!=50)?((x<50)?(4.0/100*x):(10.0/100*x)):500;

(e) Name any two tokens of java.

Question 3

(a) What are the different keywords that checks the visibility of a member of the class? What are they called?

(b) Determine how many times loop will be executed and print the output.

```
int a=1, b=2; while(++b<6)a*b;
System.out.println(a);
```

(c) Attempt the following:

(i) A package that is involved to manipulate character as well as String?

(ii) Name a data type that can hold 16 bit unicode characters.

(iii) What is the output of code below:

```
char c = 'A';
int m = 5;
System.out.println(char(c+m));
System.out.println(c+m);
```

(iv) Write statements to show how finding the length of a character array char[ ] differs from finding the lengths of string object str.

(v) Give the output of the following functions System.out. println("MALAYALAN".indexOf('A')+"Sidharth".lastIndexOf('h'));

(vi) double a = Math.pow("200".indexOf('0'),2);

System.out.println(a);

(vii) Differentiate between linear search and binary search.

(viii) Evaluate the following expression:

int p, k= 8,m=11,r=7;
p = (r++%7)+(−−m%5)+k*(++k−8);

SECTION B   (60 Marks)

Attempt any four questions from this Section

The answers in this Section should consist of the Programs in either Blue J environment or any program environment with Java as the base. Each program should be written using Variable descriptions/Mnemonic Codes such that the logic of the program is clearly depicted.

Flow-Charts and Algorithms are not required.

Question 4

Write a program in java to input a number and check whether it is a pronic number or Heteromecic number or not.

Pronic number: A pronic number, oblong number, rectangular number or heteromecic number is a number which is the product of two consecutive integers i.e n(n+1)

The first few Pronic numbers are:

0,2,6,12.20,30,42,56,72.

Question 5

Write a program to input a word from the user and remove the duplicate characters present in it.

Example:

input: crcricicket

output: criket

Question 6

Write a program to accept a sentence and print only the first letter of each word of the sentence in capital letters separated by a full stop.

e.g.

INPUT Sentence: Sid is a cricket

output: S.I.A.C

Question 7

Write a program to accept name and corresponding age in two different single dimensional array. Display the records in descending order of age using bubble sort.

Question 8

Write a menu driven program to find area of an Equilateral triangle, an isosceles triangle and a scalene triangle as per the users choice.

(i) Equilateral triangle $= A = \dfrac{\sqrt{3}}{4} a^2$

(ii) Isosceles triangle $= 1/2 * b*\sqrt{a^2 - b^2}/4$

(iii) Scalene triangle $= \sqrt{s(s-a)\,(s-b)\,(s-c)}$

Question 9

Define a class to overload a function Sum() as follows:

(i) int Sum(int a, int b) – with integer arguments a and b.

Calculate and return sum of all even numbers in the range of a and b.

Sample input: a = 4 , b = 16

Sample output: sum = 4 + 6 + 8 + 10 + 12 + 16

(ii) double Sum(double n) – with one double argument n. Calculate and return the product of the following series:

sum = 1.0*1.2*1.4*...*n

(iii) int Sum(int n) – with one integer argument n. Calculate and return sum of only odd digits of the number n.

Sample input: n = 43961

Sample output: sum = 3 + 9+ 1=13

SOLUTION SAMPLE PAPER 12

SECTION A   **(40 Marks)**

Answer 1

(a) Reusability feature is related to inheritance in java where derived class can use the methods and common data from the base class.

(b) double r1= (−b + Math.sqrt(b * b − 4 * a * c)) / (2 * a);

double r2 = (−b − Math.sqrt(b * b − 4 * a * c)) / (2 * a);

(c) (i) break;

(ii) continue
```
for(int i =1; i<10; i++)
 {
 if(i*3 == 9)
 break;
 }
for(int i =1; i<10; i++)
 {
 if(i%2 == 0)
 continue;
 System.out.println(i);
 }
```

(d) Math.cos(b)

trim().

(e) When the array is initialized during the run time of program its called dynamic initialization of array. E.g.

int a[ ] = new int[10];

Answer 2

(a) (i) m and y

   (ii) a and b.

(b)

Constructor	Method
Automatically called during the creation of the object.	Class Object needs to explicitly call the member functions.
It bears the same name as that of class.	It doesn't have same name.

(c) a=50 b=30

(d) if(x!=50)
```
    {
    if(x<50)
    amount = 4.0/100*x;
    else
    amount = 10/100*x;
    }
    else
    amount = 500;
```

(e) variables and constants.

Answer 3

(a) private, public, protected

(b) 3 times 60

(c) (i) java.lang

   (ii) byte

   (iii) F 70

   (iv) array.length and str.length()

   (v) 8

   (vi) 1.0

(vii)

Linear Search	Binary Search
It compares each element of the array with rest of the elements in the array.	It's based on divide and conquer rule. Array is sorted in this search. Element is searched only in the selected halves.

(viii) 8

SECTION B   (60 Marks)

Answer 4

```java
import java.util.*;
class Main
 {
 public static void main(String[] args)
  {
  Scanner sc = new Scanner(System.in);
  System.out.print("Input a number: ");
  int n = sc.nextInt();
  int result = 0;
  for(int i=0; i<n; i++)
   {
   if(i*(i+1) == n)
    {
    result = 1;
    break;
    }
   }
  if(result == 1)
  System.out.println("Pronic Number."+n);
  else
  System.out.println("Not a Pronic Number."+n);
  }//end of main
}//end of class
```

Answer 5

```java
import java.util.*;
class Main
 {
  public static void main(String[] args)
   {
   Scanner sc=new Scanner(System.in);
   System.out.println("Enter a sentence: ");
   String str=sc.nextLine();
   String word = "";
   char c = str.charAt(0);
   word+=c;
   for(int i=0;i<str.length();i++)
     {
     char ch=str.charAt(i);
     boolean flag=false;
     for(int j = 0; j<word.length();j++)
       {
       if(ch==word.charAt(j))
         {
         flag = true;
         }
       }
     if(flag == false)
     word+=ch;
     }
   System.out.println(word);
   } //end of main
 }//end of class
```

Answer 6

```
import java.util.*;
class Main
 {
  public static void main(String[ ] args)
   {
   Scanner sc=new Scanner(System.in);
   System.out.println("Enter a sentence: ");
   String str=sc.nextLine();
   str = " " +str;
   str = str.toUpperCase();
   String word = "";
   for(int i = 0; i < str.length(); i++)
    {
    char ch = str.charAt(i);
    if(ch == ' ')
     {
     word+=str.charAt(i+1)+".";
     }
    }
   System.out.println(word);
   } //end of main
 }//end of class
```

Answer 7

```
import java.util.*;
class Main
 {
  public static void main(String[ ] args)
   {
   int temp;
   String temp1;
   String a[ ] = new String[15];
```

```
int age[ ] = new int[15];
Scanner sc = new Scanner(System.in);
System.out.println("Enter a 15 names and their ages:");
for(int i =0; i<a.length; i++)
  {
  System.out.print("Enter name"+ (i+1) +":");
  a[i] =sc.next();
  System.out.print("Enter age"+ (i+1) +":");
  age[i]=sc.nextInt();
  }
for(int i = 0;i<age.length; i++)
  {
  for(int j =0; j<age.length−i−1;j++)
    {
    if(age[j]<(age[j+1]))
      {
      temp = age[j];
      temp1 = a[j];
      age[j]=age[j+1];
      a[j] = a[j+1];
      age[j+1] = temp;
      a[j+1]=temp1;
      }
    }
  }
for(int i =0; i <a.length;i++)
  {
  System.out.println(a[i]+"\t"+age[i]);
  }
  } //end of main
}//end of class
```

Answer 8

```
import java.util.*;
class Main
 {
 public static void main(String[ ] args)
  {
  Scanner sc = new Scanner(System.in);
  int n;
  float a,c,s,b;
  double area;
  System.out.println("1.Area of equilateral triangle");
  System.out.println("2.Area of isosceles triangle");
  System.out.println("3.Area of scalene triangle");
  n=sc.nextInt();
  switch(n)
   {
   case 1:
   System.out.println("Enter side of an equilateral triangle");
   s=sc.nextFloat();
   area=Math.sqrt(3.0*s*s)/4.0;
   System.out.println("Area="+area);
   break;
   case 2:
   System.out.println("Enter the side and base of isosceles triangle");
   a=sc.nextFloat();
   b=sc.nextFloat();
   area=b/4.0*(Math.sqrt(4.0*a*a−b*b));
   System.out.println("Area="+area);
   break;
```

```
    case 3:
    System.out.println("Enter the 3 sides of scalene triangle");
    a=sc.nextFloat();
    b=sc.nextFloat();
    c= sc.nextFloat();
    s= (a+b+c)/2;
    area=Math.sqrt(s*(s-a)*(s-b)*(s-c));
    System.out.println("Area="+area);
    break;
    default:
    System.out.println("Wrong choice");
    }
  }//end of main
 }//end of class
```

Answer 9

```
import java.util.*;
class Main
 {
 public int sum(int a, int b)
  {
  int sum= 0;
  for(int i=a; i<=b;i++)
   {
   if(i%2==0)
   sum+=i;
   }
  return sum;
  }//end of sum
 public double sum(double n)
  {
  double prod=1.0;
  for(double i =1.0; i<=n; i+=0.2)
```

```
  prod*=i;
  return prod;
  }
public int sum(int n)
  {
  int sum = 0;
  int a = n;
  int digit;
  while(a>0)
    {
    digit = a%10;
    if(digit%2!=0)
    sum+=digit;
    a=a/10;
    }
  return sum;
  }
public static void main(String args[ ])
  {
  Main s = new Main();
  System.out.println(s.sum(1, 5));
  System.out.println(s.sum(10.0));
  System.out.println(s.sum(10935));
  } //end of main
} //end of class
```

Variable	Data Type	Description
n	int	Users input integer value
result	int	Flag to check pronic number
c	char	To store first character
flag	boolean	To check character is present in word or not
str	String	User input string.
word	String	Modified string
a[ ]	string	To store 15 names
age[ ]	int	To store integer number
temp	int	Temporary variable for swapping
temp1	String	Temporary variable for swapping
n	int	Users choice
a c s b	float	S = side of equilateral triangle A b side and base of issocless triangle A b c sides of scalene triangle
area	double	To store area
prod	double	Store product of decimal number in series
digit	int	To store digit of number

www.ingramcontent.com/pod-product-compliance
Lightning Source LLC
Chambersburg PA
CBHW051052050326
40690CB00006B/696